G BEAR ACCEPTS TREATY BUT NOT A RESERVE 1
: BIG BEAR'S BAND CAMPS AT FROG LAKE NEAR A
SERVE THERESA GOWANLOCK   FROG
ARCH 19: SASKATCHEWAN   OVIS
MENT MARCH 26: BATTLE O DUCK LAKE MAR
L OF PROVISIONAL GOVERNMENT MOVES MÉTIS
CHE HOLY THURSDAY APRIL 2: KILLINGS AT FROG
RIDAY APRIL 3 FROG LAKE HOSTAGES ABSORBED
R'S CAMP MANN FAMILY ARRIVES IN FT PITT APR
OR DICKENS SENDS OUT COWAN, LOASBY AND
T FOR BIG BEAR APRIL 14/15: CREE SIEGE OF FT
SHOT; NWMP ESCAPE APRIL 17: HOSTAGES FROM F
TO FROG LAKE APRIL 19: THEY REACH THE CAMP
-GEN T.B. STRANGE LEAVES CALGARY FOR EDMO
6: FR LEGOFF AND CHIPEWYAN BAND ARRIVE
CAMP MAY 1: STRANGE ARRIVES IN EDMONTO
AMP AND HOSTAGES MOVE TOWARD FRENCHMAN
: CREE LEAVE FROG LAKE PROCEEDING FOR FR
TTE TO JOIN POUNDMAKER; RIEL SURRENDERS M
E SETS UP BASE AT FT PITT M   STRANGE A
THE ALBERTA FIELD FOR   LEAVE FT PITT FOR FR
TTE MAY 28 BATTLE OF FRENCHMAN'S BUTTE; HOS
AWAY FOR SAFETY; FR LEGOFF AND PEOPLE DESER
ANLOCK, DELANEY, PRITCHARD AND NAULT ES
N. ESCAPES SEPARATELY JUNE 2: MCLEANS AND
EACH LOON LAKE; STEELE IN PURSUIT JUNE 3: BAT
KE; GOWANLOCK AND DELANEY RESCUED BY SCOU
LEFORD JUNE 4: STEELE MEETS UP WITH MIDDL
Y; PURSUE CREE WHO FLEE LOON LAKE JUNE 7:
EPARATE FROM PLAINS CREE BAND AND STRIKE
CLEANS JUNE 9: MIDDLETON ORDERS WITHDRAWA
KE BACK TO FT PITT JUNE 18: MCLEANS RELEASE
EASED HOSTAGES ARRIVE AT FT PITT JULY 2: BIC
ANIED BY HIS SON, HORSE CHILD, AND A COUNCILO
ALF, SURRENDER AT FT CARLTON TO NWMP SGT
VADING THE NWMP FOR 200 MILES NOVEMBER 16

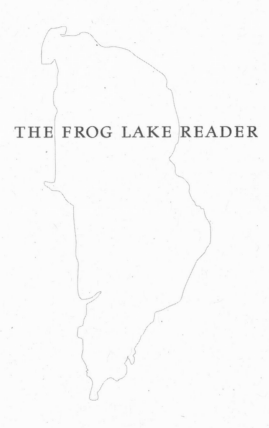

THE FROG LAKE READER

the

FROG LAKE

READER

edited and with a preface by

Myrna Kostash

NeWest
PRESS

Library and Archives Canada Cataloguing in Publication

The Frog Lake reader / Myrna Kostash, editor.

Includes bibliographical references and index.
ISBN 978-1-897126-46-2

    1. Frog Lake Massacre, Frog Lake, Alta., 1885.
I. Kostash, Myrna

FC3215.F765 2009   971.05'4   C2009-902363-6

COPYRIGHT © MYRNA KOSTASH 2009

NeWest Press acknowledges the support of the Canada Council for the Arts, the Alberta Foundation for the Arts, and the Edmonton Arts Council for our publishing program. We also acknowledge the financial support of the Government of Canada through the Book Publishing Industry Development Program (BPIDP).

Editor for the Board: Don Kerr
Cover and interior design: Natalie Olsen
Text Editor: Eva Radford
Permissions Coordinator: Mary Trush
Author photo: David Cheoros

Every effort has been made to obtain permissions for excerpts. If there is an omission or error, the publisher would be grateful to be so informed. See the Permissions section for more information.

NeWest Press
#201 8540-109 Street
Edmonton, Alberta T6G 1E6
780.432.9427
www.newestpress.com

TABLE OF CONTENTS

PREFACE

While doing the research for my book, *Reading the River: A Traveller's Companion to the North Saskatchewan River* (2006), I visited the National Historic Site of Fort Battleford, Saskatchewan. Here I learned of the only mass hanging in Canadian history, of eight First Nations men on November 27, 1885. From a tourist brochure I read in a café in North Battleford, showing a map of the town and its places of interest to visitors, I learned of the site of their mass burial, not far from the fort. I found the site, and there read on a placard that some of the men had been hanged for killings at Frog Lake, April 2, 1885. Their grave has been rededicated and it is a very beautiful but also solemn and mournful place. So is the Provincial Historic Site of Frog Lake solemn and mournful, for it contains the graves of some of those killed on April 2, 1885.

I did not pursue the story at the time, as Frog Lake was not located on the North Saskatchewan River. But in the course of my research over the next several months, I kept coming across the story, for it also involved events at Fort Pitt, Frenchman Butte, and Steele Narrows (all historic sites in Saskatchewan). I kept a separate file of these accounts; I also looked for literary texts and in new histories. The first fruit of these materials was a radio documentary I wrote for the CBC radio program *Ideas*, "Voices from Frog Lake" (2005). The next was an article in *Legacy* magazine (Summer 2008), "Following Big Bear." But even these formats were not enough to contain all that I had found and continued to find.

The fact is that an astonishing amount of material has been written since 1885 about the events precipitated by what has been known historically as the Frog Lake Massacre. Besides eyewitness accounts and contemporary press reports, people have written memoirs (in English and French), poems, short stories, novels; they have assembled oral histories; they have interviewed elders; they have rewritten the histories. All manner of perspective, voice, bias, style, is present. And so I decided to bring them all together, in excerpts, in *The Frog Lake Reader*. More than a textbook or anthology of these voices, the *Reader* works as a drama of interplaying, sometimes contradictory, often contrapuntal, narratives.

Besides the excerpts themselves, I have included edited portions of the four interviews I conducted for the *Ideas* documentary, with historians Sarah Carter, Heather Devine, and Blair Stonechild, and with novelist Rudy Wiebe. And I have added my own point of view here and there, introduced by the letters, MK.

ACKNOWLEDGEMENTS

Over the course of researching several adaptations of the literature of the 1885 Frog Lake troubles — for print and radio — I was fortunate to have the assistance and support of Duane Burton, indefatigable research associate and sound recorder; Bob Hendriks, historian in Heinsburg, AB, for difficult-to-find information about the Frog Lake area; Wayne Brown, writer in Peck Lake, SK, for a guided tour of Steele Narrows, and his wife Marilyn for hospitality in their B&B in Lakeview; Sarah Carter, Heather Devine, and Rudy Wiebe for their willingness to keep on talking about Frog Lake. Thanks to Sarah Carter for a helpful reading of the manuscript. I am grateful, too, for the professionalism and open enthusiasm of the NeWest Press staff in support of this book: Lou Morin, General Manager, Tiffany Foster, Production Editor, Diane Cameron, Marketing Assistant, Loretta Ludwig, Office Administrator, and Natalie Olsen, Designer. Thanks also to Diane Bessai, Don Kerr, and Peter Kirchmeir, for their help in the early stages, and to the NeWest Editorial Board for their decision to publish *The Frog Lake Reader*.

Myrna Kostash
May 2009, Edmonton

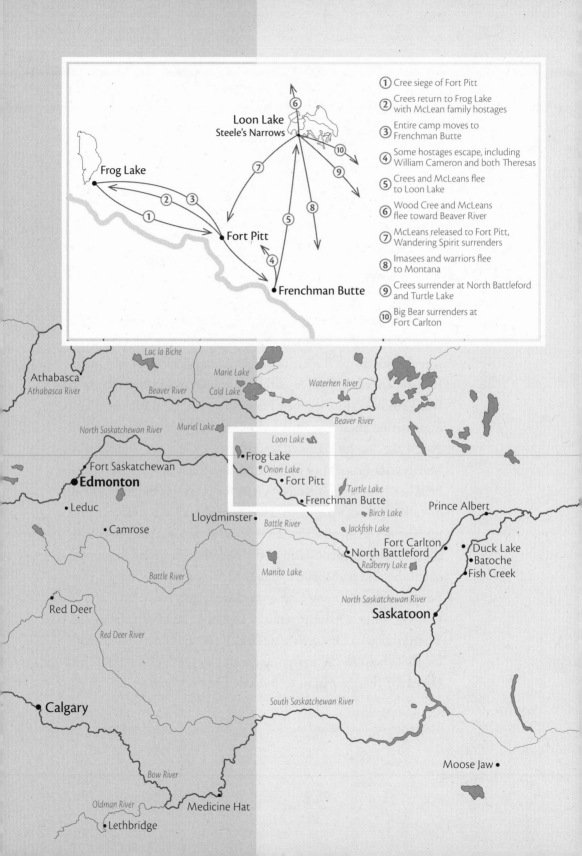

Loon Lake
Steele's Narrows

Frog Lake

Fort Pitt

Frenchman Butte

① Cree siege of Fort Pitt

② Crees return to Frog Lake with McLean family hostages

③ Entire camp moves to Frenchman Butte

④ Some hostages escape, including William Cameron and both Theresas

⑤ Crees and McLeans flee to Loon Lake

⑥ Wood Cree and McLeans flee toward Beaver River

⑦ McLeans released to Fort Pitt, Wandering Spirit surrenders

⑧ Imasees and warriors flee to Montana

⑨ Crees surrender at North Battleford and Turtle Lake

⑩ Big Bear surrenders at Fort Carlton

Athabasca
Athabasca River

Lac la Biche

Marie Lake

Waterhen River

Beaver River

Cold Lake

North Saskatchewan River

Muriel Lake

Beaver River

Loon Lake

Fort Saskatchewan

Frog Lake

Edmonton

Onion Lake

Fort Pitt

Leduc

Frenchman Butte

Turtle Lake

Lloydminster

Battle River

Birch Lake

Prince Albert

Camrose

Jackfish Lake

Fort Carlton

Manito Lake

North Battleford

Duck Lake

Redberry Lake

Batoche

Red Deer

Battle River

Fish Creek

Red Deer River

North Saskatchewan River

Saskatoon

Calgary

South Saskatchewan River

Moose Jaw

Bow River

Oldman River

Medicine Hat

Lethbridge

CAST OF CHARACTERS

Individuals mentioned in cited texts.

Big Bear (Mistahimaskwa): **Plains Cree chief, 1825–88.** Troubled by the hunger of his people due to the disappearance of the buffalo, by the encroachment of settlers on Cree lands, and by fears of poverty and cultural loss on the reserves, Big Bear refused to sign Treaty Six in 1876, determined to wait until treaty promises were kept. But in the winter of 1884, with the last buffalo gone and with the threat of mass starvation hanging over his band, he and his people moved to the Frog Lake area. By 1885, however, the young warriors, led by his son Imasees (Bad Child, Wild Child, Mean Boy) and Wandering Spirit (Kapapamahchakwew), effectively wrested control from Big Bear, which led to the killings at Frog Lake settlement in April 1885. Still counselling peace, Big Bear surrendered at Fort Carlton on July 2, 1885. He was tried for treason-felony, found guilty, and sentenced to three years at the Stony Mountain Penitentiary. He was released on March 4, 1887, and died on Poundmaker reserve a year later.

Peter Blondin: **Métis man from Duck Lake, temporarily employed at**

Gowanlock's mill, taken along with hostages into Big Bear's camp.

Jimmy Chief: **Grandson of Chief Seekaskootch, who signed Treaty Six at Fort Pitt 1876 for the Onion Lake Band. His mother was a daughter of Little Bear, who told him the story of the events of 1885.**

John Delaney: **Farm instructor at Frog Lake, from Ontario.**

George Dill: **Freetrader and storekeeper at Frog Lake, originally from Ontario.**

Mary Dion: **Mother of Joseph Dion and one of his informants in *My Tribe the Crees*.**

François Dufresne: **Worked for Tom Quinn, Indian agent at Frog Lake, when the Northwest Rebellion began in 1885.**

Father Adelard Fafard: **Oblate missionary at Frog Lake.**

William Gilchrist: **Clerk to John Gowanlock.**

Charles Gouin: **Métis carpenter with Frog Lake Indian Agency.**

Louis Goulet: **Métis mail carrier for surveyors, who cut and squared timber on government contract. Present at Frog Lake during the killings, he was one of the Métis who protected the female hostages. Interviewed by Guillaume Charette in 1903.**

John Gowanlock: **Owner and operator of grist mill in Frog Lake.**

Imasees: **Son of Big Bear, he challenged his father's leadership; after Big Bear's surrender at Fort Carlton, Imasees fled to Montana, where he changed his name to Little Bear.**

Kamistatum / Kamistatin / Baptiste Horse: **Wood Cree man who worked in the HBC store at Frog Lake and witnessed the events of 1885.**

Little Bear: **Plains Cree chief convicted of the murder of George Dill.**

George Mann (wife Sarah): **Indian agent and instructor at Onion Lake from 1879 to 1900, he and his family were taken hostage by the Big Bear band.**

Father Félix Marchand: **Oblate missionary from Onion Lake.**

McLean family: **W. J. McLean, father, was a Scot involved in the fur trade at Fort Qu'Appelle and Fort Pitt; his wife, Helen Murray, belonged to an illustrious Métis family that had been active in the fur trade for generations; they had twelve children, of whom Amelia was the eldest. W. J., along with his children Duncan, Elizabeth (Eliza), and Katherine (Kitty), all wrote versions of their experiences as hostages in the band of Big Bear.**

Sir Frederick Dobson Middleton: **Army and militia officer dispatched to the Northwest where he defeated the Métis forces at Batoche, May 15, 1885. He led an unsuccessful pursuit of Big Bear.**

Misehew: **Son of Chief Seekaskootch, who signed Treaty Six in 1876 and was killed at Steele Narrows in 1885.**

Alexander Morris: **Lieutenant-Governor of the North-West Territories (1872–76), he was involved as the Queen's representative in treaty-making with the First Nations. On behalf of the Crown, he signed treaties three, four, five, and six, over a territory spanning lands between Lake Superior and the Rocky Mountains.**

André Nault (nephew of Louis Riel), Adolphus Nolin: **Métis woodcutters in Frog Lake area, worked occasionally for John Delaney.**

Old Keyam: **"Representative character" created by Edward Ahenakew to articulate the "feelings and outlooks of Indians who have reached** a certain stage in acquiring 'Canadian civilization'" (Ahenakew, 51). Old Keyam grew up on a reserve, was sent away to school by the missionaries, but returned to become a storyteller.

Poundmaker (Pihtokahanapiwiyin): Adopted son of Chief Crowfoot, chief and orator at Battleford reserve, peacemaker at Battle of Cut Knife Hill, May 1885, against troops of Lieutenant Colonel William Otter.

John Pritchard: Métis interpreter at Frog Lake, wife Rose Delorme.

Thomas Quinn: Irish-Sioux Indian subagent at Frog Lake, wife Jane (Owl Sitting) from Big Bear's band.

Margaret Quinney: Trapper and granddaughter to Simon Gadwa (a Wood Cree scout at the time of the Frog Lake troubles), and an elder from Frog Lake.

Reverend Charles and Mrs. Quinney: Church of England missionaries at Onion Lake.

Hayter Reed: Indian agent in the Battleford District and assistant Indian commissioner for Manitoba and the North-West Territories in May 1884; member of the North-West Council.

Louis Riel: Métis spokesman, leader of 1885 Resistance in the Northwest.

Mrs. Joseph Sayers Sr., née Mary Rose: Daughter of John Pritchard, the Frog Lake interpreter, she was twelve years old in 1885 and was interviewed in 1961 by Jean Goodwill.

Seekaskootch (Cut Arm): Chief at Onion Lake reserve.

Peter Shirt: Orphan adopted by Peter Erasmus from a Peigan reserve in 1863; devout Christian, hunter, and trapper.

James K. Simpson: HBC post manager and trader at Frog Lake, wife Catherine.

Wandering Spirit (Kapapamahchakwew): **War chief and hunter in band of Big Bear.**

John Williscraft: **Lay assistant to Father Fafard.**

ONE: BEGINNINGS

George F.G. Stanley, historian: "For centuries the western prairies were the 'happy hunting ground' of these Indian tribes [Cree, Blackfoot, Blood, Piegan, and Sarcee]. Numberless herds of bison moving over the plains provided them with all the necessaries of their simple life: food, clothing and shelter. From the Rio Grande to the Peace River, the plains trembled under the heavy tread of these wild cattle. It was the golden age of Indian freedom. In the Canadian North-West the red man lived in savage opulence, wandered over the plains, hunted the 'thundering herds' and warred among themselves. The passing years brought little change to their mode of life. But, with the coming of the white man, undismayed by demons or distance, all this underwent a change" (Stanley, *The Birth of Western Canada*, 197).

MK: In his inimitable style as historian-romancer of the Canadian Northwest, Stanley sets the stage for the dramatic, fateful, and often violent encounter of First Nations hunter and European settler, a much more disruptive intruder into the plains than the people of the fur trade had been. Settlers meant permanent occupation of the plains and the impossibility of sharing them with

Big Bear (Mistahimaskwa): Plains Cree chief in 1886. Photo taken at Stony Mountain penitentiary. (Glenbow Archives NA–1315–17)

I

buffalo herds and hunters, who initially regarded them with an unfriendly eye.

Big Bear [Mistahimaskwa], Plains Cree chief: "We want none of the Queen's presents; when we set a fox-trap we scatter pieces of meat all round, but when the fox gets into the trap we knock him on the head; we want no bait, let your Chiefs come like men and talk to us" (in Stanley, 212).

MK: But, by signing the treaties made at forts Carlton and Pitt in the year 1876, the Cree chiefs acknowledged that they did in fact wish to negotiate an alliance with the government in Ottawa over the question of "ownership" over some 120,000 square miles (310,798 sq KM) of their ancestral patrimony: land. For several years now their people had been ravaged by smallpox, starvation, and the disappearance of the buffalo, up to then their sole support as a community. In a letter dated April 13, 1871, W.J. Christie, the chief factor at Edmonton House, who had been visited by a group of Cree chiefs, wrote to Lieutenant-Governor Adams George Archibald of the North-West Territories, warning that, with the extermination of their food supply, the Cree would "help themselves" to the provisions of forts and settlements.

W.J. Christie, HBC factor: "And there being no force or any law up there to protect the settlers, they must either quietly submit to be pillaged, or lose their lives in the defense of their families and property…. I think that the establishment of law and order in the Saskatchewan District, as early as possible, is of most vital importance to the future of the country and the interest of Canada, and also the making of some treaty or settlement with the Indians who inhabit the Saskatchewan District" (in Morris, *Treaties of Canada*, 169–70).

MK: Formerly employed in the negotiating of treaties three, four, and five (southeastern Manitoba and Lake of the Woods, southern Saskatchewan, and Lake Winnipeg areas, respectively), Alexander Morris, the new lieutenant-governor of Manitoba and the North-West Territories, was despatched once more to negotiate treaty, this time with the Plains and Wood Cree, at forts Carlton and Pitt, in August 1876. Negotiations with the "anxious and distressed" Indians proved difficult and protracted, but eventually all parties seemed satisfied by their agreement, according to Morris. Even though in the government view the Cree had relinquished title to the whole of the plains, they were assured they would receive instruction in farming and the support of missionaries and teachers.

Alexander Morris, treaty negotiator: "They were anxious to learn to support themselves by agriculture, but felt too ignorant to do so, and they dreaded that during the transition period they would be swept off by disease or famine — already they have suffered terribly from the ravages of measles, scarlet fever and small-pox. It was impossible to listen to them without interest.... I closed by stating that, after they settled on reserves, we would give them provisions to aid them while cultivating, to the extent of one thousand dollars per annum, but for three years only, as after that time they should be able to support themselves" (Morris, 185–6).

MK: Then Sweet Grass, called by Morris the principal chief of the Plains Cree, rose, and in words appropriate to the gravity and decorum of the occasion, told Morris he was glad to have a "brother and a friend who would help to lift them up above their present condition." He expressed his gratitude for the terms of the treaty, and, holding out his hand which he pressed against

Morris' heart, his other hand pressed on his own breast, he said: "May the white man's blood never be spilt on this earth. I am thankful that the white man and red man can stand together. When I hold your hand and touch your heart, let us be as one; use your utmost to help me and help my children so that they may prosper" (in Morris, 191).

Alexander Morris: "I will speak to you frankly, as if I was talking to my own children; the sooner you select a place for your reserve the better, so that you can have the animals and agricultural implements promised to you, and so that you may have the increase from the animals, and the tools to help you build the houses etc. When you are away hunting and fishing, the heat of the sun and the rain is making your crops to grow. I think you are showing wisdom in taking a place away from here, although it has been your home. It is better for the Indian to be away a little piece from the white man" (Morris, 244).

MK: Alexander Morris' account of these negotiations and his evident satisfaction in their conclusion have only ever provided one side of the story. For the other side, how the chiefs felt, we have only Morris' word for it. But a new generation of scholarship does give us a perspective into the motivation of the First Nations in granting the Canadian government access to their territory. They were not acting only out of desperation. As Saskatchewan historians Blair Stonechild and Bill Waiser argue, "What mattered above all else during the negotiations, was the belief that they were establishing a special relationship with the Canadian government, consisting of two equal parties who stood to benefit mutually from the agreement." In the chiefs' minds, the mutuality and the equality between the two parties were the guarantee of their future, "in the expectation that Ottawa would fulfil its responsibilities and help them make the transition to the new agricultural economy and a more secure future. They were wrong" (Stonechild & Waiser, *Loyal till Death*, 28).

John Horse, Cree informant: "[My father] Kamistatim was among those who were at Fort Pitt on September 9, 1876, where Chief Tus-tuk-ee-skaws signed Treaty No. 6. Kamistatim shook hands with the Queen's Representative. He heard many promises that were made to the native people. The Honourable James McKay and Peter Erasmus were the interpreters. He obtained the original flag that was used at the signing. This flag, that was later given to Kimowankapo [John Horse], was meant to strengthen those promises that Kamistatim heard, and to show that the laws of the Treaty would never be broken. The Queen's Representative promised by the sun and the river that as long as the sun passes and the river flows the promises would last. Because the sun and the river were created by God, if one of the promises were broken it would be a promise broken to God" (Horse, *Land of Red and White*, 67).

MK: However, in a move that would have fateful consequences for the people of the Northwest, white and First Nations, the Plains Cree chief Big Bear, along with several other chiefs, refused to sign the treaty; holding out for more concessions from the government and hoping for allocation of contiguous Cree reserves, he preferred to take his chances with hunting the last of the great bison herds grazing around the Cypress Hills, Fort Walsh, Wood Mountain, and into Montana. Unlike the Wood Cree who hunted small game in the forests, the Plains Cree hunted mainly on the open prairie, and they had no choice but to hunt further and further south as the buffalo receded from the plains down to the American boundary and beyond. That, or starve.

By 1879, with hunger intensifying, only Big Bear still refused to sign Treaty Six. But when, in the summer of 1881, no buffalo at all appeared north of the US–Canada boundary, Big Bear conceded that he could no longer feed his people, and in December 1882 signed adhesion to Treaty Six.

George F.G. Stanley: "The passing of the old days of the North-West cannot be related without a word of sympathy for the Indians. To them the old life meant independence and liberty; the new, restriction and bondage. It is a matter of no wonder that a strong stand was made against the government's efforts to make them leave their old haunts, places associated with the memories of freedom and plenty. To leave behind the tawny hills and treeless prairie was to break forever with the scenes of their happiest thoughts, and to destroy the last hope, to which they had so fondly clung, of once more being able to live by the chase" (Stanley, 236).

John S. Milloy, historian: "When the end finally came, as it did in 1879, it was heralded by a tragic cry which went up and echoed across the plains.

> *I have nothing to eat,*
> *I am dying of thirst —*
> *Everything is gone!*
> *My father, have pity on me!*

"Turning to face the east, the Cree could see the emptiness of their lands. The great herds now ran only in their memories. All that was real was the approaching European and the strange confinement of the reserve.

"If there is a tragedy in Plains Cree history, it is not that a growing dependence on white influences caused the society to crumble; rather, it is that Plains Cree society, or at least the Cree ability to organize on economic and military lines, remained remarkably unchanged, outliving the herds upon which the society physically existed. What was led into the bondage of the reserves was not the ruin of a political and social system, but rather a healthy organism which had taken root and grown strong on the plains. The fate of the Plains Cree nation followed that of the buffalo — not to death, but into a white man's pound, the reserve" (Milloy, *The Plains Cree*, 121).

Amelia M. Paget *née* McLean, linguist and author: "**Perhaps few realize how hard it is for our Indians to have to beg for the common necessities of life. They are naturally very proud and reserved, and among the older ones to beg is most humiliating. Being brought up to look upon everything as for the 'common good,' it is hard for them to have to remind people by begging that they are in want. There is, as a matter of fact, no such word in either the Cree or Saulteaux languages as 'beg.' The only thing approaching such a word in their language is 'Puck-oo-she-twan' (Share with me)**" (Paget, *The People of the Plains*, 44).

MK: The situation was exacerbated by bureaucracy: the Department of Indian Affairs, the Department of the Interior, and the Indian Commissioners for Manitoba and the Northwest, all had a hand in administration, none of it co-operative. Under the Indian Act, Indian agents administered the reserves with powers to control the bands' movements, expenditures, and agricultural equipment and resources. With the famine crisis of 1879, Ottawa appointed an Indian commissioner, Edgar Dewdney, and sent him to the Northwest, under instructions to direct the operation of the competing agencies "in such a manner as to ensure the carrying out of all treaty stipulations and covenants in good faith and to the letter" (in Stanley, 228).

In the summer of 1883, Big Bear and his band moved north to the district of Fort Pitt on the North Saskatchewan River. When he saw what life on the reserve was like, he resisted accepting a settlement. Early in 1884 Deputy Superintendent General of Indian Affairs Lawrence Vankoughnet had cut back on the department's budget for rations, arguing this would encourage the Cree to take up their reserves. Government-issued food rations had been cut to the Indians on the reserves; local Indian agents no longer had independent authority to distribute vouchers, and even the Wood Cree who, unlike the buffalo hunters of the plains had been farming their reserves for some time, went hungry for lack of a market for their grain, or even a mill.

Once confined to the reserves, it was hoped by government that the Indians, "discouraged" from using tents and tipis, would build houses and barns, send their children to the schools that would be built there, and receive instruction in raising cattle and planting potatoes. But, in fact, the reserve economy consisted mainly of relief and a policy of work-for-rations. According to historian Sarah Carter, the work-for-rations policy was "a mean-spirited act since the amount of food provided was not only well below caloric needs but sometimes unfit for human consumption" (in Stonechild & Waiser, 37). As for schools, from 1883 they were built away from the reserves as residential industrial institutions and under the control not of government but of religious foundations. Tribal governance was gradually supplanted by the local Indian agent. Resistance to this system on the part of the old chiefs, writes Stanley, "was resented by the Government and denounced as noxious and heathenish.... The chiefs and head-men became mere names, archaeological expressions" (Stanley, 241). Likewise "heathenish" were the ritual dances, which were "discountenanced" by the withholding of "any gift of provision" when not outright suppressed.

Walter Hildebrandt, poet: *"Reed, Major Hayter ... Entering the outside service of the Dept. of the Interior, 1881, he became Indian Agent, Battleford Dist., and Asst. Indian Comnr. for Man. And N.W.T., May 1884. Apptd. a mem. of the N.W. Council, Apl., 1882, he served as Admnr. of the Govt. of the N.W.T., Feb., 1884, and, afterwards, as Comnr. of Indian Affairs and Depty. Supdt. Genl. of Indian Affairs, being apptd. to the latter office, Oct., 1893. He remained in that office till placed on the retired list, 1897.... elected Presdt. of the Ottawa Polo Club, 1896.*

> - "Indians called him 'Iron Heart' (it was said he liked that)
>   [...] — Questioning the system was not permitted
> - he thought the Indian childlike
> - he refused to negotiate compromise or concession
> - ignored established traditions on treaty day
> - Indian complaints he saw as attempts to avoid work
> - 'work for rations' policy was thus rigorously enforced
> - his mission no work no food [...]
> - earned the label Iron Heart refusing rations no matter
>   how piteous the plea"
>   (Hildebrandt, "Marginal Notes," 40–1)

MK: The choice had been cruel: famine on the empty hunting grounds, or penurious settlement on a reserve.

Winter 1883–84: driven by hunger and near-destitu-tion, some Indians stole food and assaulted government farm instructors. Government eased up on some of its restrictions but, for the peace-minded among the Cree, notably the old chief Big Bear, it was too late. Their authority had been undermined by the agents and now the young warriors, Big Bear's son Imasees, Little Poplar, and Wandering Spirit [Kapapamahchakwew] asserted their leadership. The severity of the winter of 1884–85 pushed them to the point of hoping to join up with the Métis in Saskatchewan, led by Louis Riel in armed insurrection.

Alexander Morris: "There is another class of the population in the North-West whose position I desire to bring under the notice of the Privy Council. I refer to the wandering Half-breeds of the plains, who are chiefly of French descent and live the life of the Indians. There are a few who are identified with the Indians, but there is a large class of Metis who live by the hunt of the buffalo, and have no settled homes ... and while I would not be disposed to recommend their being brought under the treaties, I would suggest that land should be assigned to them ..." (Morris, 295).

Heather Devine, historian, interview: "First of all it should be remembered that by the time Treaty Six was negotiated, the government was aware that there were three classes of mixed-race people living in the Northwest. And Alexander Morris, who was the lieutenant-governor of Manitoba and the North-West Territories and the man responsible for negotiating numbered treaties three to six, drew distinctions between these different groups of mixed-race people.

"When the government negotiated Treaty Six they chose not to make any provision for other groups of Métis, they just chose to negotiate treaty and include those mixed-blood people who were culturally 'Indian,' to take treaty, as Indians.

"And, because Treaty Six is essentially a Cree treaty, you've got a number of culturally Cree, mixed-bloods taking treaty. And the reason for that is that, historically, the Cree had the closest working relationship with Europeans due to the fur trade. And because of the fur trade relationship, there's a lot of intermarriage. So it's not surprising that you've got large numbers of mixed-race Cree people taking treaty."

MK: In the early 1880s, almost everyone living in Canada's Northwest had grievances against the Government of Canada in Ottawa. First Nations people, who had signed treaties and moved to reserves, were angry about the government's failure to live up to its commitments. White settlers protested their lack of political representation and the dominance in Ottawa of eastern-Canadian interests. The Métis, descendants of First Nations and European marriages, were desperate for Ottawa to recognize their rights of possession to their farms along the Saskatchewan in advance of the inexorable influx of settlers who were already beginning to fill up agricultural land — right behind the surveyors. The CPR and the Hudson's Bay Company had received vast tracts of land from the federal government and, of course, the First Nations had been granted reserves. Yet the government delayed surveying the land and issuing scrip (a certificate issued by the government that could be exchanged for land). Even white settlers were sympathetic to their plight — or were at least anxious about their own security in the event of organized Métis protest.

In May 1884, a group of whites, English-speaking mixed-bloods, and French-speaking Métis held a protest meeting near Prince Albert and determined to seek famed Métis champion Louis Riel to lead their cause. At St. Laurent, on March 8, 1885, another meeting passed a ten-point Bill of Rights that included the demand that "this region be administered for the benefit of the actual settler, and not for the advantage of the alien speculator."

David Breen, historian: "**By the autumn of 1884 the desperate plight of the northern Indians was clearly apparent.** Observing that on almost all the reserves the crops had failed, C.B. Rouleau, the federal agent who had been sent to Battleford to investigate half-breed grievances, urged that increased provisions of food and clothing be distributed by the Indian agents to alleviate the 'misery and starvation' that he predicted would be accentuated during the coming winter. The great danger, he warned, was that a hard winter would unite the Indian and Métis against the government. Rouleau advised Dewdney, Lieutenant-Governor of the North-West Territories, that the Métis grievances should be settled quickly, for 'once the half-breeds quiet, there is no possibility of any union between them and the Indians, and the latter being isolated will be always easily controlled'" (Breen, "Timber Tom," 1).

MK: To make matters worse, the crop in the fall of 1884 was a failure due to near-drought. Every settler and inhabitant felt the pressure of immediate want and need. As a sympathetic observer of the community, the teacher Robert Jefferson reported: "Every variety of wild talk was indulged in at these meetings and very few had either the will or the courage to dissent.... As Ottawa appeared unmoved by all these declamations, the thoughts of all turned to Riel" (Jefferson, *Fifty Years on the Saskatchewan*, 123).

Robert Jefferson, adventurer and teacher: "**Since there were Halfbreeds at Duck Lake who could write and others scattered over the country** who were able to read, it is quite understandable that natives in all parts of the country were kept tolerably well informed as to the progress of the agitation at headquarters. These men have been called spies of Riel, but it is difficult to see that they were anything more or less than people who had an interest in the result of the movement and kept in touch with what was going on" (Jefferson, 154).

Louis Goulet, mail carrier: "[Riel delegate] Gabriel Dumont ... reminded us of the fact that, when the Governor General of the Dominion had come to the West in 1878, the Métis had set out their griev-ances for him. They'd told him they never received any land grants as the Manitoba Métis had, by virtue of their Indian ancestry. Not only that, even those who had been settled on farms for fifteen, twenty years and more had never received rec-ognition of their titles, and the government agents made them pay for hay and wood they cut on lands which they thought should belong to them twice over, once as natural children of the country by right of their Indian birth and again by right of settlement and occupancy.

"Gabriel Dumont spoke for a long time about the miseries and injustices the Métis had endured ever since the day they'd let the White men set themselves up as lords of the land.

"In conclusion, Dumont told us: 'And let me tell you, my friends, that's not the end of it. The government will never give us anything! They stole our land with promises and now they've got control, they're laughing at us. They don't intend to grant us the slightest thing in return for soil where gen-erations of our ancestors sleep. No. We'll never get anything from them, until we take matters into our own hands and force the government to give us justice'" (in Charette, *Vanishing Spaces*, 110).

G. Mercer Adam, author: "The sedition of Riel was the signal for the rising of this mass of disaffection ['no less than five thousand' Indians on the North Saskatchewan]. His runners carried news of the half-breed revolt throughout the district, and the Indian nature could not resist the contagion" (Adam, *From Savagery to Civilization*, 302).

MK: Into this brew of disaffection was poured the suspicion on the part of government authorities that Big Bear was behind the growing talk of "sedition." It was the view of the Indian agent for the Battleford District, Major Hayter Reed, that "Big Bear is an agitator and always has been" and that with the "moral support" of the Métis behind him, he could be expected to "incite" the Indians (in Stanley, 293–4). Historians and journalists writing at the time accused him of being a "malign influence" on his restless people (Adam, 302) and of summoning all the bands in his vicinity to pow-wows in order "to persuade all within his reach of influence to dig up the hatchet, abandon their reserves, and under his wild, savage and reckless leadership to demand his rights, and the fulfilment of the promises that had been made him — at the muzzles of their rifles, or at the edge of the scalping-knife" (Mulvany, *History of the North-West Rebellion*, 121).

Blair Stonechild, historian, interview: "They needed someone to demonize and he [Big Bear] made a good target. He had first run afoul of white authorities by questioning the Treaty Six negotiations. He was very hesitant about simply accepting the motives of the commissioners, with the result that he didn't sign, and it was many years before he did. He had a reputation as someone who was a resister, someone who was a difficult politician, in the sense that he wasn't easily convinced and was very skeptical. And so he was conveniently an individual who could be easily transformed into this 'monster', though it's very clear from the writings that he was a very spiritual and principled individual.

"And what [our book] was an effort to do, was an effort to show that First Nations leaders did have a position. In fact, they did debate and think about what their actions should be in the Northwest Rebellion, that, in fact, there were movements afoot particularly on the part of Riel to implicate them, and actions were taken to bring about their involvement."

MK: In June 1884, Big Bear rode to Poundmaker's reserve near Battleford where he sponsored a Thirst Dance, a traditional spring ritual, according to Blair Stonechild and Bill Waiser, "representing renewal and cooperation." Residents of Battleford, however, feared it as the "warm-up to an eventual Indian rebellion" (Stonechild & Waiser, 56). But there were also skeptics, such as P.G. Laurie, the editor of the only newspaper in the North-West Territories, the *Saskatchewan Herald*, whose tone was condescending; but he had also made a penetrating observation — that among the disaffected Cree and Métis there was no "unanimity." And there would be none, in the ensuing events of 1885.

P.G. Laurie, newspaperman: "There is no truth in the report of a past or probable rising of the Indians in this district, nor any other that we know of. The noble red man may try to intimidate an odd storehouse keeper, and in an emergency capture a bag of flour or a side of bacon; but as to a general uprising, he has strong reasons for letting that job out. He has neither horses, without which he cannot move; nor arms and ammunition, or any means of buying them; nor has he any provisions to carry him over campaigning; above all there is an absence of unanimity among the bands such as is necessary to insure success in case of conflict with whites" (in Stobie, *The Other Side of Rebellion*, 29).

Blair Stonechild, interview: "I don't want to second guess the decision that [First Nations] leaders made back more than a hundred years ago, but what I can tell you is that the historical relationship between First Nations and non-First Nations people went back to 1670 when the fur traders arrived on the shores of Hudson Bay, and that there was a trading relationship which thrived and existed over several hundred years. Certainly this relationship was not perfect and there were certainly unjust things that happened, but by and large the two sides had decided that they could mutually benefit from each other's existence.

"The chiefs who negotiated the treaties in the 1870s were looking for peoples with whom to live side by side in friendship and partnership. As a matter of fact, the language of the treaty itself is one which is similar to how one talks about a family relationship. This was the premise that the leaders were working on at the time of the Rebellion. I know that virtually no chiefs supported Riel. Those who supported him were generally those who sympathized with the Métis. And of course it's hard to judge those individuals because there was a real sense that government was not living up to the treaties, there was a sense that there was a betrayal of the treaties."

Peter Shirt's dream, March 1884: "I have had an odd dream that bothers me a lot ... I dreamed that a very old man came to me and, taking me by the hand, led me to the top of a high hill. 'Look to the east,' he said, 'and tell me what you see.'

"'I see many black clouds churning and rolling in many

queer shapes and forms. Yet they seem to cover the same area and are not drifting with any wind. What does it mean?'

"'It means that there will be war and bloodshed and troubled times for many people'" (in Erasmus, *Buffalo Days and Nights*, 271).

TWO: TROUBLE AT FROG LAKE

MK: On a miserable June day in 2005, with the heavy overcast sky threatening rain and a relentless wind ploughing through the aspen bush, I stood at the site of the so-named Frog Lake Massacre of 1885 — or, rather, stood at the little cemetery not far from the site where lie buried seven of the men killed on April 2, 1885, in the early weeks of the Northwest Rebellion.

In what is now Alberta, hard by the border with Saskatchewan, in the parkland near the North Saskatchewan River country near the reserve of Frog Lake First Nation, I meandered shoulder-high in grass and bramble, wild rose bushes and aspen deadfall. I noted the still-visible slumps of land where cellars had been dug for the houses and Hudson's Bay Company post of the settlement of Frog Lake. The calm beauty of the fields spread out all around belied the violence and tragedy commemorated here.

A monument, a very imposing stone cairn about two metres high, erected by Historic Sites and Monuments Board of Canada in 1926, describes the event as a "massacre" by "rebel Indians under Big Bear" who then also "took prisoners." Among these prisoners, or hostages, were the widows of two of the men killed, as well as a young employee of the HBC, William Cameron, all of whom eventually wrote about their ordeal, held for two months in the camp of Big Bear and his people and followers. They were sometimes terrified by their captors but ultimately they also shared their anxiety and privation as they trekked cross-country just several kilometres ahead of militias in hot pursuit.

William Cameron, HBC clerk: "The Cree nation is divided into two branches, Wood and Plains Cree. The former — whose property these reserves were — differed widely in character and mode of life from their brethren of the plains. They were solitary hunters and trappers afoot, the mainstay of the Saskatchewan valley fur trade....

"The Plains Crees, on the other hand, pitched their lodges in the great open territory between the North and South Saskatchewans.... They were better orators, more crafty, savage and daring than were their relatives of the woods" (Cameron, *Blood Red the Sun, xxii*).

Old Keyam, storyteller: "The Treaty had been made in due and proper form. There had been justice, apparently, and kindliness too on the part of those who represented the Crown. Yet at the signing there were men, both white and Indian, who were sick at heart because they knew the almost certain outcome, yet could see no alternative.

Old Keyam is a character created by Edward Ahenakew to represent the generation that grew up in the aftermath of the events of 1885.

"In those days before the Rebellion, the reserve at Frog Lake seemed to be developing. The Indian Agency was there, and an outpost of the Hudson's Bay Company from Fort Pitt. There was a mill too, run by water-power. Everything is gone now, only the cellars remaining, and a heavy wheel from the mill.

"The Chief of the [Frog Lake] reserve was *Chas-cha-ki-s-kwas*

(Head-upright), and he and his band were Bush [Wood] Cree, a quiet and peaceable group. But there were five bands in all encamped at Frog Lake, each under its own Chief. The Plains Cree under Big Bear were long used to bloodshed, brought up from childhood to regard battle as the highest test of their manhood, ever at war with the Blackfoot and the Bloods in a feud that meant killing at sight, in the quickest and most practical manner ... The winter had been severe, and with so large an encampment the hunting was difficult. The presence of Big Bear's band fostered discontent and resentment ..." (in Ahenakew, *Voices of the Plains Cree*, 73-4).

William Cameron: "Frog Lake, a shimmering expanse of blue water, lies ten miles north of the North Saskatchewan river, with which it is connected by a creek bearing the same name ... The settlement — to dignify it by the name — lay at the foot of the lake. There were the buildings of the government Indian agency, the Hudson's Bay Company trading post, the Roman Catholic mission, and the store of a 'free' trader named Dill. On the creek, two miles away, a dam under construction marked the site of a small grist mill waiting to be built for the Canadian Indian Department. The contractor, John C. Gowanlock, lived with his young wife in a log house on the bank of the creek nearby, and his clerk, William C. Gilchrist, lodged with his employer" (Cameron, *xxii*).

Allen Ronaghan, historian: "Fathers [Leon] Fafard and [Joseph-Jean-Marie] Lestanc had assisted in the founding of St Jean-François Regis Mission at Fort Pitt in 1877.... It soon became clear, however, that, with the disappearance of the buffalo, Fort Pitt no longer enjoyed a central position in the movements of the Native peoples. In the early 1880s, St. Jean-François Regis was closed and a new mission — Notre Dame de Bon Conseil — was begun at Frog Lake.... Here Father Fafard worked with his customary zeal; by 1885 this mission was something of a showpiece in the Catholic outreach system. There was a church, two houses, a school with a good library, a stable, three horses, a plough, a buckboard, a farm wagon and a cart.... The school was so successful that Father [Felix] Marchand was sent to help Father Fafard" (Ronaghan, "Who Was the 'Fine Young Man'?", 16–7).

G. Mercer Adam: "John Delaney, the Farm Instructor, had in 1882 come with his wife from the neighbourhood of Ottawa, and had the supervision of four bands of Indians in proximity to Frog Lake. His official duties were also to attend to the issue of Government rations to the followers of Big Bear. We are told that he was engaged in the performance of this humane duty when the outbreak took place. A like beneficent work had brought Mr. J.A. Gowanlock to Frog Lake: he was engaged in erecting a mill for the benefit of the Indians of the district" (Adam, 305–6).

Richard Laurie, surveyor: "Frog Lake ... was one of the points apparently selected for a centre for teaching the Indians farming when a number of farming instructors were sent from Eastern Canada in 1878.... In the summer of 1884 the Indian Department advertised a bonus for anyone who would build a grist mill at Frog Lake. Mr Gowanlock,... being a practical millwright, suggested to me to go in with him, and take up the proposition. ...While working on the framework of the dam, I received a letter from Mr Gowanlock that he would be bringing a wife back with him and to build him a house" (Laurie, *Reminiscences of Early Days*, 20–2).

Mel Dagg, author: "The truth is she has been married two months to a man moving fast on the far edge of frontier, a man who combined their honeymoon with a trip east to buy machinery and then left her waiting six weeks in Battleford.... Her eyes follow the cold green river coiling and uncoiling through the bare trees. She searches the valley below, wondering what is across the bridge, on the other side, the wilderness that claims her husband and from which he will soon return to take her to Frog Lake ..." (Dagg, *The Women on the Bridge*, 47–8, 39).

Theresa Gowanlock, wife of John Gowanlock: "Another time on going out [in Battleford] while two men were crossing the bridge over Battle river; a horse broke through and was killed and the squaws gathered around it taking the skin off, while others carried some of the carcass away, and I asked what they were going to do with it, and my husband said 'they will take it home and have a big feast ...'" (Gowanlock, *Two Months*, 6).

Mel Dagg: "The three women bend over the horse and she glimpses the flash of their knives as they fall upon the mare.... They hurl away the hooves and the head, and fling the intestines in an arc that ends with a splash in the water below.... In less than twenty minutes all evidence of the horse and the women is gone and it is possible to believe for just a moment that she did not see the slaughter, that it didn't happen.... On the bridge between settlement and wilderness, she has glimpsed a part of the country she had not known existed" (Dagg, 39–40).

Theresa Gowanlock: "That little settlement of our own ... was distant from the Frog Lake Settlement, our nearest white neighbours, about two miles. But we had neighbours close by, who came in to see us the next day, shaking hands and chatting to us in Cree, of which language we knew but little. The Indians appeared to be very kind and supplied us with white fish twice a week" (Gowanlock, 10).

Theresa Delaney, wife of John Delaney, (from Deposition given at Regina): "My husband and I left home [County of Carlton, Ontario] 1ˢᵗ of August 1882, and went at once to Frog Lake, NWT, where my husband held the position of Indian Instructor.... He then had to look after the Chippewans, Oneepowhayaws, Misstoos, Kooseawsis, and Puskeaskeewins and last year he had to ration Big Bear's tribe. He was so engaged when the outbreak took place. All these Indians were peaceably inclined and most friendly to us all. My husband was much respected, and really beloved by all under his care, and they seemed to be most attached to him" (in Mulvany, 400–1).

George Stanley [Mesunekwepan], grandson of chief of Frog Lake Reserve: "One day (in 1884) a man named Ouche came over and told my father [Chief Ohneepahaow] that a white man — a Government man — had come to Onion Lake the day before and was coming to Frog Lake to meet the Indians that day.... The Government man said; 'I have been sent here on very important business to you.... Big Bear wants to come here with his band to camp over the winter [1884/5].... I would be very glad if you would give him permission.... He will have to cut some wood on your land, catch some fish in your lake, etc. but for this you will be paid by the government.... There is one more thing I want to speak about.... I wish to find out from you if the Indians will be willing to let the white people build a grist mill at Frog Creek.'... The mill was proceeded with and a store built nearby which had big windows on the south. Big Bear and his band came from the south in the Fall and camped about two miles south of our camp" (in Hughes, *The Frog Lake Massacre*, 159–60).

William Cameron: "The months of January and February passed uneventfully. Big Bear and his band were camped in the timber along Frog Creek not far from the mill site.... The old chief often had dinner with me; thus I had frequent opportunities to study his deeply-lined, intelligent face. Big Bear was then perhaps sixty years of age. He had an amazing voice and when he talked, as he often did, with his right arm free and the left holding the blanket folded across his broad chest, with the dramatic gestures and inflections natural to him, he reminded me of an imperial Caesar and was one of the most eloquent and impressive speakers I have ever listened to" (Cameron, 26–7).

Blair Stonechild and Bill Waiser, authors: "But all was not well at Frog Lake. Although the tiny hamlet with its Indian agency, Hudson's Bay Company storehouse, Roman Catholic mission (Notre Dame de Bon Conseil), and new grist mill seemed destined for a promising future — there was even talk of a railway connection — tensions churned beneath the surface. Part of the problem were the two government officials that the Indians had to deal with on a daily basis. Thomas Quinn, the local Indian agent, was a tough-minded autocrat, who in the words of NWMP Superintendent Crozier was 'very much disliked.'... Prior to assuming his duties at Frog Lake in 1883, the slight though pugnacious Quinn had worked out of the Battleford Indian agency and assisted in moving bands in the Cypress Hills area, including Big Bear's, to the North Saskatchewan country. [By winter 1884 Big Bear's group was camped by the Wood Cree reserve at Frog Lake.] In his new position, he adhered steadfastly to the Indian department's work-for-rations policy as if it were carved in stone. Nothing could deviate him from his course — not even his Sioux heritage or his Assiniboine wife. And he quickly earned a reputation as a mean-spirited, petty little man completely lacking in compassion" (Stonechild & Waiser, 108).

C.P. Mulvany, author: "Mr T.T. Quinn, the Indian Agent, was known as one of the most capable and competent of the employees in the Indian Department in the North-West. He was born in the Red River valley, his father being an Irish trader and his mother a Cree half-breed. He received a good education at the St Boniface College. When a mere lad he went down into Minnesota and spent some time in a trader's store and it was while he was there that the Minnesota massacre occurred. His employer's store was raided and its owner murdered, but in the midst of these scenes of horror an Indian who had taken a liking to young Tom Quinn's bright and handsome face hid him under the counter among some empty salt sacks, and by that means he made his escape from savages who were sparing neither women nor children, no matter how helpless they were. As a young man Mr. Quinn entered the service of the Hudson's Bay Company in which he soon distinguished himself for courage, intelligence, industry and thorough honesty" (Mulvany, 96–7).

G. Mercer Adam: "Thos. Quinn, the trusted Indian Agent of the Government, was a native of Red River. His father was an Irish traveller in that region, and his mother a Cree half-breed. Physically, Quinn was a fine speciman of humanity: he was a thorough frontiersman and accomplished horseman, and an expert canoeist. He is said to have laboured long and zealously for the conversion of his Pagan brethren and to have earnestly sought the amelioration of their condition" (Adam, 305).

Louis Goulet: "Tom Quinn and George [sic] Delaney knew from experience that as soon as the land had been cleared it would be much in demand for homesteads, once the Indians had been removed to their reserve. They were cooking up a plan to clear land before it was opened for settlement" (in Charette, 158).

Heather Devine, interview: "What eventually happened is that [Big Bear] held his ground. He wanted a larger land base for his band. The government wanted them to settle in another location. Big Bear did not like the terms. They go through the winter of 1884 without rations. They're living in the vicinity of the Post at Frog Lake where they do not like the people in charge. They see them as ... I guess you could call them hard-dealers, hard-nosed people. There were rumours circulating about the Indian agent sexually harassing Indian women in the area. They didn't like that."

Fred Horse, Cree elder: "[A]n agent had to be also flexible, patient and tactful. These qualities were not apparent in Tom Quinn. He was compulsively stubborn and notorious for his explosive temper. At first the Indians had given him the name, 'Sioux Speaker,' but he soon became better known as 'Dog Agent' and 'The Bully.'... Quinn was often contemptuous of Indians and enjoyed demonstrating his authority over them.... The Indians saw him as the most reluctant dispenser of food rations in the entire Department. He hoarded supplies with such tenacity and doled them out so unwillingly that one would have thought he had to pay for them himself. This was the man who would be dealing with the Big Bear Band in that perilous winter" (in Jean Goodwill, *John Tootoosis*, 48)!

Rudy Wiebe, author: "He sat back, his left hand crept into his vest, his right occasionally lifted the tea mug; he began to talk. Of his half-Sioux mother in Minnesota and his Irish-French father killed there in ambush by the Sioux while scouting for Major Brown during the massacre in 1862; of himself fighting through the Carolinas with the Wisconsin Regiment of what was now called the Grand Army of the Republic; of himself with the cavalry scouting against the Cheyenne and Arapaho (before they got smart and signed on as scouts themselves) and Sioux; of Dewdney saying they definitely needed a man like him to handle the Plains Cree" (Wiebe, *Temptations of Big Bear*, 230–1).

Old Keyam: "And I have been told by those who knew [Quinn] well that he was utterly wild and reckless, a 'no-good man,' were the words used of him. The Indians listened with more confidence to those who, like A-yi-mi-ses, Big Bear's son, urged a council meeting with the Chiefs of Onion Lake and Long Lake, who were moderate men" (in Ahenakew, 74).

Heather Devine, interview: "And they were getting impatient with their own leadership, Big Bear. They felt that he wasn't achieving anything in his negotiations. They had gone through the winter without rations, so by the time springtime arrives, they are angry, hungry, they're fed up."

William Griesbach, major general and son of a NWMP officer: "The real commander of the Indians was not Big Bear but Wandering Spirit. He was a cold-blooded individual who hated the whites like poison and had as a warrior a good deal of ability" (Griesbach, *I Remember*, 76).

"[Quinn] could not easily contemplate any challenge to his own authority, not from Big Bear, and especially not from

Wandering Spirit. The rivalry was well known" (in Goodwill & Sluman, 51).

Fred Horse: "Given the helpless and famished state of the Crees as that deadly winter wore on, gifts of food in return for favours rendered would have been irresistible and truly in keeping with the frontier morality of the time, often thinly veiled by the surface Victorian postures of virtue. As William Cameron was later to say: '...That weakness — for a tawny oval face — was a failing of too many of the white men whom the government employed to show the ignorant red man how to live'" (in Goodwill & Sluman, 54).

William Cameron: "Then too, Delaney abused his power as Farm Instructor to take advantage of Indian women. When the husband of one of the women protested, a man named Sand Fly, John Delaney trumped charges of assault against him, had him imprisoned, and then cohabited with his wife all winter. To add insult to injury, when he tired of the Indian woman, Delaney married a white woman, Theresa Delaney" (in Dagg, 111).

Hugh Dempsey, historian and biographer: "The feeling was general that 'Mr. Delaney had the man arrested in order to accomplish his designs,' and he cohabited with the prisoner's wife all winter. Sand Fly's brother, Dancing Bull, resented the actions of the autocratic farm instructor and may have become a threat, for in 1882 Delaney accused him of witnessing the killing of a government ox and saw him sentenced to four months in jail" (Dempsey, *Big Bear*, 117).

Fred Horse: "It was hunger which brought about anger to the Plainsmen. ... Their children were crying for food. They were hungry and the Indian Agent refused food" (in Stonechild & Waiser, 114).

Hugh Dempsey: "Early in January 1884, Big Bear's father-in-law, *Yayakootya-wapos*, returned from a long hunt, hungry and empty-handed. Exasperated, he went to see Delaney to beg a little food for his family. Because of [government's] strict orders [that provisions were to be given only in exchange for work], the farm instructor was forced to turn him down and brusquely ordered him to get out of the ration house. Instead, the tired and frustrated Indian sat down on a pile of frozen fish and declared he would not move until he had some food. Delaney's response was to grab him by the arm to forcibly eject him, but *Yayakootyawapos* reached under his blanket and drew his knife. Surprised and frightened, Delaney dashed for the door but had enough presence of mind to lock it on the way out. When the Mounted Police arrived a few minutes later, *Yayakootyawapos* was taken into custody and sentenced to two years in the guardhouse at Battleford. This incident was just one of many that involved hungry Indians that winter" (Dempsey, 123).

Vernon LaChance, editor: "Now they were at Frog Lake and, at latest report showed, in utterly wretched conditions, poorly clothed, and destitute of food, except when supplied with provisions by the Indian Agent there. Even the horses were suffering and several had died. No big game had been shot at Frog Lake and to obtain the necessities of life Big Bear's followers had been compelled to submit to the implications of Agent Quinn's dictum: 'No work, no food.' As a result they had reluctantly agreed to work at cutting wood" (Vernon LaChance, *Diary of Francis Dickens*, 77).

D'arcy Jenish, author: "Many of [Big Bear's] followers had no stomach for political struggle, for an endless fight against impossible odds. They simply wanted a home and whatever assistance the government might provide to help them start new lives. They had hoped Big Bear would choose a reserve after the long march north from the Cypress Hills in the summer of 1883. And they became sullen and resentful when he stalled yet again in the fall of 1884.... The camp included another faction. It was made up of warlike young men who still dreamed of riding the plains and ridding them of whites. They rallied around Wandering Spirit, Big Bear's militant war chief. In the winter of 1884–5, Wandering Spirit acquired a potent ally – the spellbinding Little Poplar, a renegade Cree who had rolled in from Montana preaching defiance and spoiling for a confrontation" (D'arcy Jenish, *Indian Fall*, 157).

Fred Horse: "Wandering Spirit had been born, had grown to maturity and earned his scars as an outstanding hunting and fighting man. He had fed, protected and served his people in the best tradition of that war-like nation. Now he could do none of those things. He had to crawl around after gophers where once he had raced amidst the thundering herds. He had been forced to watch as his children grew thin and listless and shivered in their ragged clothing.... The Plains tribes have, as always, defended their own hunting ground — theirs as far back as anyone could remember. Would white men have stood idly by, while outsiders came in and began to shoot their cattle? Not likely! It seemed that there was one law for white men and quite another for the Indians. Well, it would not happen again. There were soon no more buffalo left, either to shoot *or* defend. Wandering Spirit had been jolted out of his once honoured role, out of the only way to live that he had ever known.

He was left stranded and humiliated, subject to the grudging charity of the Indian agent" (in Goodwill, 50–1).

Fred Horse: "[Big Bear's Band] was looking forward eagerly to the October treaty payments. It was the custom to give each band enough fresh meat at that time so that they could enjoy a good feast before taking their money.... But when the Big Bear Band rode up into Fort Pitt on the date set for the payments, Tom Quinn announced that he was not going to give them any meat for the expected feast on the excuse that they had not yet co-operated with the government and chosen a reserve! Their bitter disappointment soon changed into furious outrage" (in Goodwill, 48–9).

William Cameron: "Quinn got to his feet. Six and a half feet tall, spare, athletic, broad-shouldered, exceedingly active, Thomas Trueman Quinn was a splendid figure of a man. It was from his knowledge of the Sioux language that he had received from the Crees his name of Kapwatamut or The Sioux Speaker.

"[Little Poplar] scowled: 'I have heard of you!' he retorted. 'Away over the other side of the Missouri river, I heard of you. I started to come this way and the farther I came the more I heard. You're the man the government sent up here to say "No!" to everything the Indians asked you!'

"'Now, I am going to ask you something. I will ask it three times before I sit down. It is long since the buffalo went away. My people are hungry and would like to eat fresh meat again. Will you kill an ox before the treaty money is paid?'

"Quinn shook his head. 'The government gives cattle to the Indians for work and milk, but not to kill. There's no beef for you.'

"Little Poplar went on: 'I crossed the Line and travelled north.

After a time I came to where the grass had been torn up, and two iron lines had been laid down and stretched away to the east and west as far as I could see. I said to myself, "What is this?" I thought for a moment: then I said: "Hai, yes, I know! This is the *pewabisko meskano*, the iron road that the government has made to carry food and clothing in their big wagons to the poor starving Indians.'"... He turned again to Quinn. 'For the second time I ask: Will you give us beef?'

"'I've answered that question. You heard what I said,' replied the agent.

"'*Namoya, itwayo!* No, he says. *Akwusee keeam!* Very well!' Little Poplar raised his voice.... 'For the third and last time I ask — and when you answer, *speak loud* so that every Indian in this house can hear you: Will you give us beef?'

"'*No!*' came the reply in the deep voice of the agent.

"And with yells of defiance the whole band swept out of the house [Fort Pitt], across the square and up the hill, firing their guns in the air as they went. That afternoon the Indians started the war dance and Big Bear made a speech. He attacked the government and the Hudson's Bay Company and, ignoring the other whites present, walked up to Captain Francis Dickens, son of the novelist, commanding the NWMP at Ft Pitt, and held out his hand.

"'You are a man,' cried Big Bear, 'whom Manito made to be a chief! We like you, your heart is good. As for that man' — he pointed at Quinn — 'his heart is made of stone'" (Cameron, 4–7).

Isabelle Little Bear Johns, granddaughter of Big Bear: "I was about 8 years old. My father was third son of Big Bear.... I lived with my foster parents, Mr. and Mrs. Peter Thunder and our home was amongst the other Indian houses which constituted the main camp....

"My people belonged to that great race called the Plains

Indian. We lived entirely on the buffalo who provided us with food, shelter and clothing. We were not trappers or growers of seeds, although we did obtain some of our food from edible roots and plants....

"Our men had only one means to earn food, and that was to chop wood for the river steamers in exchange for a piece of bacon or a sack of grain. There was a limit to how much firewood the Hudson's Bay steamer could use, since it sometimes made only one trip up the Saskatchewan River per season. Therefore, there were times when the men of my village couldn't chop wood for food or anything. It was at this time that our chief Big Bear organized his last big hunt" (Little Bear Johns, *Edmonton Sunday Sun*, 16).

Rudy Wiebe, interview: "**And Big Bear actually goes moose hunting, at a time when things are starting to accumulate in Frog Lake, in April, end of March 1885. Big Bear is away moose hunting. This is a buffalo hunter, away hunting a solitary moose in the bush, who's used to hunting buffalo on the plains. This is part of what's happened; their life has been taken away from them and they're back to the life they have left, because their identity is attached to the plains culture. So when Big Bear's men are starving because they can't go out on the plains, there's no buffalo left on the plains, this is partly where this conflict comes from.**"

Rudy Wiebe: "**He danced. He had not eaten buffalo for a long time and he could not rest too long for perhaps he might not be able to begin again, though the fear of that was nothing compared to the other he would not consider, and he was praying over and over as he danced, swaying only a little now, barely raising his feet to the rhythm of the ground:**

Thunder you know I promised

but bacon and flour with a few sweet fish

empty a man

thunder giver

give

give" (Wiebe, 166).

THREE: THE DUCK LAKE FACTOR

MK: SPRING 1885: March 26, near the Métis settlement of Duck Lake in what is now Saskatchewan, the first armed engagement between Métis and some Indians from nearby reserves, under the command of Louis Riel, and Mounted Police and volunteers from Prince Albert, under the command of Superintendent L. Crozier, concluded in a decisive Métis victory. The ninety-four Mounties and volunteers had marched out of Fort Carlton with a 7-pounder gun to meet the Métis forces less than a kilometre from Duck Lake. Their guns fired ineffectually over the heads of the Métis, who were sheltering behind snowbanks and brushwood, and their 7-pounder was disabled. Crozier gave the order to withdraw.

George F.G. Stanley: "The casualties in the small government force had been heavy. Ten men lay dead upon the field; two more were on the point of death and eleven had been wounded. All but surrounded, exposed to the fire of an enemy they could not see, and with five of their transport horses killed or disabled, retreat was the only sensible move.... Confusion reigned everywhere; nevertheless the retreat was effected. The Métis were

Imasees: warrior and son of Big Bear. No date available. (Glenbow Archives NA–5356–1)

37

anxious to complete the rout of their enemies, but Riel, who had viewed the battle armed only with a crucifix, declared, 'Pour l'amour de Dieu de ne plus en tuer ... il y a déjà trop de sang répandu.' Accordingly the shattered column, thus saved from annihilation, slowly made its way back to Fort Carlton, leaving behind nine of their dead and a trail of blood-sodden snow" (Stanley, 328).

Robert Jefferson: "They received the news from Duck Lake, and naturally spread around such information as came to them. As had been said before, there are many Halfbreeds who live on the Reserves and take treaty, through whom everything that happened or was expected to happen was passed on to the Indians. No spies were therefore necessary to keep Big Bear informed of events, nor did he and his band need any incitement to throw their weight on to Riel's side when they heard of the fight at Duck Lake" (Jefferson, 155).

Heather Devine, interview: "This [the victory] doesn't encourage the Indians to join the Métis cause per se; they're not particularly interested in that. What they're interested in, what they're intrigued by, is the fact that the Métis defeated the whites. And, all of a sudden, they see that the whites can be beaten."

MK: Hoping for more news, a group of Métis woodcutters at nearby Moose Lake travelled to Frog Lake.

Louis Goulet: "[Métis hunter William] Gladu showed up again at our camp on the Monday, saying, 'Well, listen here old-timers, have I got some news for you! They say the Métis beat the police at Duck Lake and the Frog Lake detachment took off last night [for Fort Pitt].' Now, what the hell could all that mean?... Things were starting to look serious.... After dinner, Dolphis Nolin, Andre Nault and I decided to see for ourselves what was going on at Frog Lake. We left on horseback about 3 o'clock.... On our way past Gowanlocks' house a mile or two outside of Frog Lake [Gowanlock's clerk William] Gilchrist informed us that Mr. and Mrs. Gowanlock were visiting Mr. and Mrs. Delaney in the village.... [W]e carried on, going through Big Bear's camp, which was divided into two parts, one on each side of Frog Creek, a mile before the entrance to the village....We carried on as far as the first house, which was Father Fafard's. We tied our horses and went in. The priest was worried, but very, very glad to see us, especially Nolin and myself. He had a lot of confidence in us as trouble-shooters. As soon as he saw me he asked if I was afraid of Big Bear's men. I told him I wasn't, adding that even though the Métis had fought and won at Duck Lake, the Indians were intelligent enough to know it couldn't go on like that for long. Besides, they wouldn't do anything to harm civilians ..." (in Charette, 115–6).

Auguste-Henri de Trémaudan, historian: "As soon as he learned of the Métis uprising, Big Bear assembled his best warriors, holding *pow-wow* after *pow-wow* where the Indians went over and over again their grievances against the Canadian government, its agents, and of the Hudson's Bay Company and its employees for unfair treatment. 'Not only were the foodstuffs and other goods of poor quality, but they were in short supply and what there was was very expensive. No matter that the furs which the trappers brought in under the treaty obligations might have been of incomparable richness, [HBC trader James] Simpson and his assistants always found them neither good nor beautiful enough. In this way, the merchants treated the Aboriginals with contempt and had only scornful words and shabby treatment for them. The dogs of the post were better treated than the Indians.'

"Thus spoke Big Bear" (Trémaudan, *Histoire*, 315; MK trans.).

Hugh Dempsey: "That night, Big Bear's warriors slipped away from their lodges and assembled along the west side of the lake, where [war chief] Wandering Spirit and Little Bear had pitched their teepees. 'Pretty soon other people started to come across,' recalled Little Bear's grandson, 'and camped all around them. Then they started to build a place for a war dance and when it was finished they started to dance. While the dance was going on, Wandering Spirit got up and said, "Quiet! Tomorrow I am going to eat two-legged meat [i.e., kill someone]. So what do you think" (Dempsey, 153)?

William Cameron: "I closed the trading shop early and with my skates under my arm walked over to Frog Creek, intending to skate down to Gowanlock's.... I had not skated two miles before I was thoroughly wet and decided to go ashore and walk back to the settlement. The trail took me through Big Bear's camp. The band was in council.... I noticed the tense, serious looks on the faces of the warriors smoking the long stone pipe round the fire in its centre as I entered the lodge. I saw at once that this was no ordinary social affair.... The talk was of 'news.' Wandering Spirit, the war chief, rose and spoke earnestly in his low, impassioned voice and with that transfixing look in his dark eyes that I have never seen in those of any other Indian.... I knew all the Indians well, for I had met them almost daily at the trading post during the winter. But I saw that I was not altogether welcome and I soon left" (Cameron, 28–9).

Mel Dagg: "He had thought he knew them, but he only knew that part which they had chosen to reveal, allowing him to think he was on familiar terms for their benefit, a facade of friendly banter across the counter of the Bay store for the young clerk when they wanted something. He had assumed he was in control, but it was *they* who were in control ..." (Dagg, 63).

Old Keyam: "The day before the outbreak of violence was quiet except for the business of preparing for a feast and dance, yet a feeling of foreboding hung over the camps, even the dogs howling now and again as though they could sense trouble. Then the dancing began, and though it was not a war dance there was bound to be recklessness where so many young men were gathered. Everyone who has told me of the tragic happening has said how the excitement and restlessness mounted steadily, until by midnight it was truly alarming.

"The first real act of hostility came in the early morning when a young Indian took a horse that belonged to one of the white men. Then the young men began to race at full speed about the encampment, yelling as they rode, more and more out of control" (in Ahenakew, 74).

Theresa Delaney: "When one sees, for the first time, these horrid creatures, wild, savage, and mad, whether in that war-dance or to go on the warpath, it is sufficient to make the blood run cold, to chill the senses, to unnerve the stoutest arm and strike terror into the bravest heart" (Delaney, 69).

Francis Dickens, NWMP inspector: "Mr. Quinn said that he would remain at his post; the Farm Instructor Mr. Delaney said the same; Mrs. Delaney then said she would stay with her husband. All the others then said they would stay but insisted that the Police should leave as their presence only tended to exasperate the Indians.... Mr. Quinn again stated that all was quiet and that he did not fear any disturbance" (in Dempsey, 152).

Theresa Delaney: "I have heard it remarked that it is a wonder we did not leave before the second of April and go to Fort Pitt; I repeat, nothing at all appeared to us a sign of alarm, and even if we dreaded the tragic scenes, my husband would not have gone. His post was at home; he had no fear that the Indians would hurt him; he had always treated them well.... [H]e would never have run away and left the Government horses, cattle, stores, provisions, goods etc. to be divided and scattered amongst the bands ..." (Delaney, 68).

MK: On April 1, 1885, Big Bear's men gathered at the home of Indian Agent Thomas Quinn, accompanied by Big Bear himself, back from a fruitless hunt. The group, Indians and agent, sat in a tense silence. The former had hoped for a distribution of rations, the latter loudly refused. The HBC clerk, William Cameron, barged in.

Kamistatum/Baptiste Horse, HBC employee: "Once inside, [Cameron] found that the agent had other visitors, Big Bear, Ayimasess [Imasees] and two more Indians. The chief's face was still dark and swollen from his hunting trip and he seemed very sombre. He was telling of a dream he had once experienced in which he had seen blood spurting from the earth and when he covered it with his hand to stop it the blood spurted from another place, and when he tried to stop that one, yet another appeared" (in Goodwill, 64).

"Ayimasees, Big Bear's usually taciturn son, now made a final attempt to reason with the belligerent agent. 'Brother, let me tell you one thing. The way I think everything will work out for the best. My father, Big Bear, is poor and old. He went north to try and hunt for food. Whatever he kills, he gives to the people. He puts on a feast and feeds everybody. Maybe you should give him food from your supplies so that he could invite all the people and feed them.'... But Quinn was now beyond all reason, well into one of his famous tantrums.... 'Ayimasees, Ayimasees, I cannot give anything to your father, I will not give him anything. Why should I give him anything?... I am not going to give you people anything to eat!'

"These words sealed the fate of Frog Lake" (in Goodwill, 61).

Louis Goulet: "Then Tom Quinn came over from his house which was about two hundred yards from Father Fafard's. If ever I saw a man spooked, it was him! Just like the others, he asked what we thought of the situation and we gave him the same answers. Tom Quinn was a Sioux Métis whose father had been killed in the 1862 massacre in Minnesota. He was a very big, very strong man who treated the Indians with arrogance and brutality. That morning I reminded him that now was a good time to put on a good face because the Indians are always brave in front of somebody who shows fear. I was able to calm him down a little, but he still had his ears laid back" (in Charette, 116)!

Rudy Wiebe, interview: "Quinn is a man in power who exercises his power in quite dreadful ways. He quite arbitrarily says — as it seems to them — 'today you have flour, tomorrow you don't have any more flour.' Because he is in a power position, he controls the food supply, which is the most dangerous thing because it is the most essential thing for people who don't have resources to hunt. So, Quinn may be a very good government agent, but a terrible government agent as far as Native people are concerned."

MK: The two missionaries at Frog Lake, Marchand and Fafard, tried to mediate.

Auguste-Henri de Trémaudan: "The two Oblate missionaries of the area, Father Felix Marchand, who came from the diocese of Rennes, and Father Leon Fafard, of the diocese of Montreal, did their best to calm people's spirits, but the principles of religion had not penetrated very deeply in the Indian and as a consequence had little influence" (Trémaudan, 315; MK trans.).

Rudy Wiebe, interview: "I have been a historical novelist all my life. As a novelist I use exactly the same sources as historians use. In *Temptations of Big Bear* I decided I wasn't going to invent any character at all; I was going to try to use only the character that history gives us and tell his particular story, but in fiction. That way, I can range from the facts, including into the heads of characters and give you their thought processes while something is happening. A historian is not supposed to do that.

"It was Big Bear's attempt to control his warriors and not kill anyone, to not fight, because fighting was the worst possible thing you could do, which appealed to me tremendously. I am a pacifist who feels war never gets you anywhere, that killing is the worst thing you can do. What you want to do is talk, talk, talk. And that's what Big Bear wants to do with the white men. He wants to keep talking with them. But the warriors at a certain time say, 'No, we've finished talking, there's no more point in talking, they [the white men] have to be done away with.'

"The other point to this is that Big Bear actually talks a great deal and he tries to negotiate. But, of course, talking leaves no record, except in the minds of the talkers. The record of the peace negotiator, of the person who tries to negotiate peace, in a sense disappears. So it's necessary for us to reconstruct [that record], if we take seriously the fact that there were people present — and the leading one was Big Bear — who were trying to negotiate. But if you have two stubborn people — Thomas Quinn, the Indian agent, and the war chief who was at the head of some very powerful and aggressive and overwrought young men — talking at a certain point breaks down. And that's what happened at Frog Lake."

John Gowanlock (left) and John Delaney (right).
Taken from 1999 edition of *Two Months in the
Camp of Big Bear* (see Works Cited).

FOUR: KILLINGS AT FROG LAKE

Fred Horse: "The story I am about to tell is during the time the Indian people were living here in the Frog Lake area. My father used to tell me, 'Some day in the far-off future people would want to know this story; I may not live to see that day.' That day has come. Now that my father has gone, I am being asked to tell this story. He did not tell me the story only once, but he used to repeat it on many evenings, and sometimes during the day. This is why I know it as well as I do. I even know exactly where all the buildings stood, the way my grandfather told it. I know where all the bodies were. Nobody really knew what happened, this is why the story was never told" (in Goodwill, 39).

Heather Devine, interview: "The problem that exists right now with mainstream Canadian understandings of the events at Frog Lake is that there have been sweeping generalizations made about the people who were actually involved in this event and the circumstances under which these events took place. I'll be more specific about that. This so-called massacre has been laid at the feet of the Plains Cree, most of whom were involved peripherally, rather than directly, in the 1885 Rebellion. In fact it was a small group that was part of one Cree–Ojibwa band that was responsible for the events at Frog Lake. However, most of the Cree people of northern Alberta and Saskatchewan have had to deal with the stigma associated with this event, rightly or wrongly.

"The other problem with the events at Frog Lake is that they occurred contiguously with the battles that occurred elsewhere in the 1885 Rebellion. In the popular consciousness, the 1885 events are known as the Riel Rebellion. Therefore, the events at Frog Lake, which came about by the actions of a small group of Cree settling some scores with the Indian agent and other people — events which took place partially due to the effects of drugs and alcohol and resentment — have also been used to implicate the Métis, who were not specifically involved in that particular event but who have had to pay the price for that event along with the actual Cree who were punished for it in the end."

MK: The cemetery at the historic site of Frog Lake is enclosed by a stout iron fence, and centred by a large stone cairn. Everything outside the fence is pretty much parkland bush, but we know that here, on either side of this cemetery, stood the Frog Lake settlement. If you cross the little road away from the official site, you can make out a wooden turnstile almost lost in the bush but which gives access to what had been part of the original settlement. Knee-deep in bush and brambles, grasses, and wild rose bushes, you are hard-pressed to imagine the village of Frog Lake which, on April 2, 1885, according to popular parlance, became a "scene from hell."

Rita Feutl, journalist: "Talk to anyone in this sparsely populated area 200 miles east of Edmonton, and they'll tell you the same thing.

The massacre that took place here had little, in the beginning, to do with Riel's Northwest Rebellion. Or for that matter with the Indians of the Puskiakewinen and Onipoheous Reserves, more commonly referred to as the Frog Lake Band.

"Francis Dufresne, who lives next door to Frog Lake on the Fishing Lake Metis Settlement (population is just under 500), insisted the Metis played no role in the massacre. 'It was the Indians who did it.' 'Yes it was,' agrees Margaret Quinney, in her home on the Frog Lake Indian Reserve, which counts less than 1,000 people as its members; but it wasn't the Indians *from* the reserve who committed the murders. 'They ought to call it the Big Bear Tribe's Massacre,' she said emphatically" (Feutl, *Edmonton Sun*).

John G. Donkin, NWMP constable: "**Frog Lake** is a lovely sheet of water lying amid groves of trees and surrounded by beautiful meadows. It is about thirty miles from Fort Pitt, and some ten miles from the Saskatchewan. Here a corporal and five men of the Mounted Police had been stationed during the winter. After the fight at Duck Lake, Inspector [Francis] Dickens recalled his men from this outpost, and also advised the whites to come into the fort [Pitt]. There was a church and a village, but on every side were treacherous redskins under that old scoundrel Big Bear. On the receipt of tidings that hostilities had broken out, they at once went on the war-path in all the hideousness of semi-nudity and paint" (John Donkin, *Trooper*, 139).

Richard Laurie: "I pulled out of Frog Lake about the 8th of March and little did I dream that I was seeing the last of my friends and of the prosperous little settlement as on April 2nd all the white men were massacred and their buildings burned....

"[T]here was not a suspicion that any trouble was brewing

but as news of Riel's agitation at Batoche and finally the result of the Duck Lake fight became known the Indians of Big Bear's band became more offensive in their actions. Big Bear's son, Masees [Imasees], and Wandering Spirit, were the leaders of the malcontents. There being only six policemen among the hundreds of Indians Agent Quinn thought it better that they should return to Pitt as their presence was a source of irritation to the Indians" (Laurie, 24, 26).

Alphonse Dion: "Inspector Dickens informed Indian Agent Quinn of the uprising and advised him to come to Fort Pitt immediately. Quinn refused, saying the Indians were quiet and he could handle them.... The police were dispatched from Frog Lake on March 31, 1885" (in *Land of Red and White*, 68).

Louis Goulet: "Wednesday evening [April 1] ... Tom Quinn still couldn't make up his mind [about leaving for Fort Pitt]. Noticing how he seemed to want to travel in the evening, rather than the day, I got the impression he was afraid.... At daybreak the next morning I was awakened by the faint sound, echoing from the ground, of a horse at full gallop: 'Hey! That's Nolin.' Soon as he arrives, he leaps off his horse. 'Zat you, Louis?' — Yes. — Well, mon gars, an Indian just told me I should get the hell out of here right now, if not sooner. They're up to no good this morning. Everything's all set; no use trying to save anybody, just enough time to save our own skin if we don't want to have to sew it back on'" (in Charette, 117)!

MK: As the plaque on the cairn erected by Historic Sites and Monuments Board of Canada, 1926, describes it: "North-West Rebellion, Frog Lake Massacre. Here on April 2 1885, rebel Indians under Big Bear massacred" — and a list of those killed follows.

If you turn away from the cairn you see two rows of orderly black crosses, marking the graves of seven of the dead. This is not where they died; they died several metres away from this site, but they were finally buried here under direction of the federal government. The crosses read: *John Delaney, massacred 2nd April 1885; John Gowanlock, massacred 2nd April 1885; John Williscraft, massacred 2nd of April, 1885; William Gilchrist, massacred 2nd of April 1885;* and then we move to the second row. *Charles Gouin, massacred 2nd of April 1885; Thomas Quinn, massacred 2nd of April 1885; George Dill, massacred 2nd April 1885;* and then under a stone of his own, inscribed by the Royal Canadian Mounted Police, Constable D.L. Cowan who was in fact killed at Fort Pitt and reburied here along with the others fallen at Frog Lake. Fathers Marchand and Fafard were buried by the mission church at Onion Lake and reburied later at St. Albert Mission.

Theresa Gowanlock: "The first news we heard of the Duck Lake affair was on the 30th of March. Mr. Quinn, the Indian Agent at Frog Lake, wrote a letter to us and sent it down to our house about twelve o'clock at night with John Pritchard [Métis interpreter for the government Indian agency], telling my husband and I to go up to Mr. Delaney's on Tuesday morning [March 31], and with his wife go on to Fort Pitt, and if they saw any excitement they would follow. We did not expect anything to occur. When we got up to Mr. Delaney's we found the police had left for Fort Pitt. Big Bear's Indians were in the house talking to Mr. Quinn about the trouble at Duck Lake, and saying that Poundmaker the chief at Battleford wanted Big Bear to join him but he would not, as he intended remaining where he was and live peaceably…. We all went to bed [the night of April 1] not feeling in any way alarmed" (Gowanlock, 14).

Theresa Delaney: "All day, the 1st of April, [the Indians] talked and held council, and finally the Indians went home, after shaking hands with my husband. They then told him that the half-breeds intended to come our way to join Riel! That they also intended to steal our horses, but that we need not fear as they (the Indians) would protect us and make sure no horses would be taken and no harm would be done.... Big Bear, himself, was away upon a hunt and only got to camp that night, we did not see him until next morning. During that day, the Indians, without exception, asked for potatoes and of course they got them. They said we did not need so much potatoes and they would be a treat for them as they meant to make a big feast that night and have a dance.... Thus we parted on the night of the first of April, and all retired to bed, to rest, to dream. Little did some amongst us [know] that it was to be their last sleep....

"At about half-past four in the morning of the 2nd of April, before we were out of bed, Johnny Pritchard and Aimasis [Imasees] came to our house and informed my husband that the horses had been stolen by the half-breeds. This was the first moment that a real suspicion came upon our mind. Aimasis protested that he was so sorry. He said that no one, except himself and men, were to blame. He said that they danced nearly all night and when it got on towards morning they all fell asleep....

"In about half an hour some twenty Indians came to the house. Big Bear was not with them, nor had they on warpaint, and they asked for our guns, that is my husband's and Mr. Quinn's. They said they were short of firearms and that they wished to defend us against the half-breeds. They seemed quite pleased and went away. An hour had scarcely elapsed when over thirty Indians painted in the most fantastic and hideous manner came in. Big Bear also came, but he wore no warpaint. He placed himself behind my husband's chair. We were all seated at the table taking our breakfast. The Indians told us to eat plenty as we would not be hurt. They also ate plenty themselves — some sitting, others standing, scattered here and there through the room, devouring as if they had fasted for a month ..." (Delaney, 65–7).

Theresa Gowanlock: "My husband and I got up and Mrs. Delaney came downstairs with a frightened look. In a few minutes Big Bear's Indians were all in the house, and had taken all the arms from the men saying they were going to protect us from the half-breeds, and then we felt we were being deceived. They took all the men over to Mr. Quinn's ... then they came back and Mrs. Delaney got breakfast. We all sat down but I could not eat, and an Indian asked Mr. Gowanlock to tell me not to be afraid, they would not hurt us, and I should eat plenty" (Gowanlock, 15).

William Cameron: "I was sleeping soundly in my room at the Hudson's Bay post. I awoke with a start. A hand, clutching my shoulder, was shaking me roughly. It was just sunrise. I sat up. Walking Horse, a Wood Cree employed about the post, stood beside the bed. His eyes were ablaze with excitement.... 'They've taken the horse from the government stables, already. They say, the half-breeds, but I believe it is Big Bear's men.' I needed no further urging. I dressed quickly and went downstairs. Immediately, Imasees entered, followed by twenty of the younger bucks. Their faces were daubed with vermillion and they carried rifles.... 'Have you any ammunition?' he asked curtly. I thought I was fortunate to be able to tell him that I had. 'Well, we want it.' ... Others reached across the counter [in the post shop] and helped themselves to the long butcher-knives on the shelves, and files with which they began to sharpen them....

"I found a messenger from Wandering Spirit awaiting me. I was wanted at the agent's house, he said. I went, under the guard of the young men he had sent. They did not behave in any unfriendly manner; simply surrounded me. There were nine white men beside myself in the little settlement, and when I reached Quinn's office I found them all seated in it. Quinn sat at the farther end with the Scotch half-breed interpreter, John Pritchard, and Instructor Delaney near him. The Indians crowded around them and blocked the doorway. Wandering Spirit held the centre of the floor. He was speaking. His manner aroused in me a distinct feeling of dismay.

"'Who is at the head of the whites in this country?' he demanded, shaking his fist in Quinn's face. 'Is it the governor, or the Hudson's Bay Company, or who?' Quinn laughed. I think he must have already abandoned any hope that he would be permitted to see another sunset; the laugh was harsh and forced.... 'Sir John Macdonald, a man at Ottawa,' he replied. 'He is the chief of all the white men who deal with the Indians.'... I know I felt at the time that the authorities were not without blame for the position in which we found ourselves. Quinn should have had a strong force of the police at his back when he was sent to deal with the most intractable band of Indians in the country" (Cameron, 43–3, 44–5).

Blair Stonechild, interview: "What I tried to point out in the book about these so-called murders was, first, an aspect that had not been included in the prevailing literature: the fact that when Wandering Spirit, and the small group of individuals that he was leading, went to the HBC store to get hold of some of the food and rations and goods there, they also came across a supply of alcohol and painkillers. And that this was something they certainly indulged in, in the hours preceding the massacre, the so-called massacre of Frog Lake. It's an obscure aspect but it did in fact occur, so that is an element that has to be introduced.

"In today's context, if you have an individual who is obviously under the influence of a number of intoxicants, are they fully in control of what they can do? So, if you look at those individuals in Frog Lake, you should take into consideration the fact that they were starving for a number of days, and they were faced with an extremely ugly situation, the political situation, the administrative situation, and that they wanted most of all to get hold of the goods and the food, so they could take it themselves."

William Cameron: "[Trader] George Dill's store stood on a hill directly before the Hudson's Bay post. They had looted it early in the morning, breaking in the doors and windows. Wandering Spirit dropped in. Since I had last seen him, he had smeared his eyelids and lips thickly with yellow ochre. He looked hideous. 'Why don't you go to the church?' he asked in his hard voice. 'Your friends are already there.' No smile played on the face of the war chief today; instead, the worst passions of his savage nature were depicted there" (Cameron, 46).

Theresa Gowanlock: "After breakfast they took us out of the house and escorted us over to the church; my husband taking my arm, Mr. and Mrs. Delaney were walking beside us. When we got to the church, the priests were holding mass; it was Holy Thursday, and as we entered the door, Wandering Spirit sat on his knees with his gun; he was painted, and had on such a wicked look. The priests did not finish the service on account of the menacing manner of the Indians; they were both around and inside the church. We were all very much frightened by their behaviour. They then told us to go out of the church, and took us back to Mr. Delaney's, all the Indians going in too [and then out again]. The Indians were going through all the stores. Everything was given to them, and they got everything they could wish for and took us up the hill towards their camp" (Gowanlock, 15).

William Cameron: "The door of the church was open ... Big Bear and Miserable Man stood inside at the back. The chief told me later he was there to prevent bloodshed and I believed him; for though outwardly calm, well do I recall the suppressed feeling and determination on the old warrior's face....

"The congregation was kneeling, and I knelt with the others. A moment later came the rattle of musketry from the door and looking out from beneath my arm I saw Wandering Spirit enter. He moved cat-like on his moccasined feet to the centre of the church and dropped on his right knee there, his Winchester clutched in his right hand, the butt resting on the floor. His lynx-skin war bonnet, from which depended five large eagle plumes, crowned his head; his eyes burned and his hideously-painted face was set in lines of deadly menace. Never shall I forget the feelings his whole appearance and action excited in me as I watched in stupefied amazement while he half-knelt, glaring up at the altar and the white-robed priests in sacrilegious mockery. He was a demon, a wild animal, savage, ruthless, thirsting for blood" (Cameron, 46–7).

Theresa Delaney: "When we arrived at the church the mass was nearly over. The Indians, on entering, made quite a noise and clatter. They would not remove their hats or headdresses, they would not shut the door, nor remain silent. In fact they did anything they considered provoking and ugly. The good priest, the ill-fated Father Fafard, turned upon the altar and addressed them. He warned them of the danger of excitement and he also forbade them to do any harm. He told them to go quietly away to their camps and not disturb the peace and happiness of the community. They seemed to pay but little attention to what they heard, but continued the same tumult. Then Father Fafard took off his vestments and cut short the mass, the last that he was destined ever to say upon earth; the next sacrifice he would offer was to be his own life. He as little dreamed as did some of the others that before many hours their souls would be with God, and that their bodies would find a few days sepulchre beneath that same church, whose burnt ruins would soon fall upon their union in the clay. The Indians told us that we must all go back to our place. We obeyed and the priests came also" (Delaney, 68).

Blair Stonechild, interview: "I think they were satisfied to keep these individuals captive initially: they took them from the church and held them captive. That was their bargaining strategy. But with the influence of the intoxicants combined with the resistance of the Indian agent, whom they despised, they ignited a situation that did not form part of their initial intention."

Theresa Delaney: "After about an hour's delay and talk, the Indians told us to come to their camp so that we would all be together and that they could aid us better against the half-breeds. We consequently started with them. Up to this point, I might say, the Indians showed us no ill-will.... We felt no dread of death at their hands, yet we knew that they were excited.... We could have no idea of the murderous intentions on the part of the Indians. Some people living in our civilized country may remark that it was strange we did not notice the peculiar conduct of the Indians.... I have heard it remarked that it is a wonder we did not leave before the second of April and go to Fort Pitt; I repeat, nothing at all appeared to us a sign of alarm" (Delaney, 68).

Theresa Gowanlock: "We had only gone but a short distance from the house when we heard the report of guns, but thought they were firing in the air to frighten us ..." (Gowanlock, 15).

Theresa Delaney: "We were followed and surrounded by the Indians. The two priests, Mr. and Mrs. Gowanlock, Mr. Gilchrist, Mr. Williscraft, Mr. Dill, Mr. Gouin, my husband and myself formed the party of whites. My husband and I walked ahead. When we had got about one acre from the house we heard shots, which we thought were fired in the air. We paid little or no attention to them. I had my husband by the arm" (Delaney, 70).

William Cameron: "The Indians were sacking the Mounted Police barracks and as I was passing it Yellow Bear came out and stopped me. Earlier in the day he had asked for a hat.... It was now 10 o'clock. 'I want to get that hat,' he said.... The shop was not more than a hundred paces distant. Half way we were stopped by Wandering Spirit. He was running, carrying his Winchester at the trail. 'I told you to stay with the other whites!' he exploded, his rifle poised suggestively in front of him as he stood for an instant regarding me darkly out of his evil eyes. Yellow Bear interposed quickly. 'He's going with me to get a hat. The sun's hot and I have none.'... Thinking over the situation since, I have reached the conclusion that the only thing that saved me at this pregnant juncture was Yellow Bear's instant grasp of my peril. Wandering Spirit had all morning endeavoured to keep me constantly with the other whites and he was now clearly exasperated by his failure to do so and as a result was ready at once to begin the massacre, as he proved to be ten minutes later.... I was locking the shop again, when Miserable Man appeared with an order from the Indian agent. I glanced across and saw Quinn standing on the hill I had just quitted, faced by Wandering Spirit" (Cameron, 48–9).

Kamistatum: "Quinn was almost back to his own house when he found it blocked by Wandering Spirit. The two men eyed each other coldly. Wandering Spirit broke the tense silence. 'Everyone is getting ready, you should be ready too so you can join the rest.' Quinn replied flatly that he was not going. It was the climactic moment in their long, long enmity. Quinn was looking into the face of death, and he must have sensed it but, perhaps, he thought he was doomed anyway, or imagined that he could pull one more bluff on Wandering Spirit. Wandering Spirit, seemingly still in control of his own anger, asked Quinn three more times in the ceremonial Cree manner to go over to the new camp and Quinn refused each time.... Wandering Spirit then said,... 'I don't know what kind of a head you have that you do not seem to understand. I may as well kill you.' He raised his 30–30 rifle and fired. Quinn spun around, then fell, his blood spilling out on the last of the winter snow" (in Goodwill, 69–70).

Rudy Wiebe, interview: "The Frog Lake murders begin with Wandering Spirit shooting Thomas Quinn. That's when it all starts, that's when it breaks loose. You have here exactly the worst possible situation. Wandering Spirit, who sees it as his duty to protect his people, is opposed by Tom Quinn's absolute refusal to move. All Wandering Spirit says is, 'Come to my camp. You are my prisoner. I am taking you prisoner, you must come to my camp.' And Tom Quinn says, 'I'm not going to do it.' What can you do in this situation if you are Wandering Spirit? You can physically overpower Quinn and take him prisoner. But Native people don't physically overpower people, they talk. They say, 'I've got you prisoner, you come with me. Either you come with me or I kill you. I'm not going to put my hands on you and drag you to prison.' This is the white man's way of doing things. Native people talk, and if you won't talk, they shoot you. That's the way a war chief behaves. If you can't convince someone to do something, then you do something drastic. But you don't pick him up and carry him to prison.

"So, when Wandering Spirit speaks to Tom Quinn — and all the witnesses agree on this — and says, 'You come with me to my camp,' and Tom Quinn says, 'No,' and Wandering Spirit asks him four times, and Tom Quinn says, 'No,' then Wandering Spirit finishes: 'I've asked you four times to do this and you're not going to do it, I can do nothing else but shoot you,' and he shoots him."

Isabelle Little Bear Johns: "On the morning of the shooting, which was a day of feast, my people could be found in small groups all over the village.... I started out with my foster mother to get flour at the agency. I carried a small tin pail because we hoped to get flour with which to make biscuits.... It all happened so quickly that I cannot say for sure what happened other than we saw Wandering Spirit raise the gun and fire at the Agent who was at the time standing in front of the Agency. Mr Quinn, who was wearing a Scottish beret, suddenly fell forward and his cap tumbled to within a few feet of where I stood. Immediately Wandering Spirit and his friend yelled, 'Let's all go in and get something to eat now.' All I remember is that I was very frightened and left my foster mother's side and ran back to our house.

I was soon to learn, however, that my people rushed into the agency and took what they needed, food, supplies and clothing. Then the building was burned.

"The instant Wandering Spirit had shot Agent Quinn, I looked at the still figure of the man lying there at the door of the agency and suddenly noticed that his hat had rolled along the ground to within a few feet from where I was standing. In my mind I thought how stubborn this little man was — for all he had to do was consent to move away to the main camp and let my people help themselves.... I heard a woman who was standing close by me saying to Wandering Spirit, 'You should be ashamed of yourself, shooting a defenceless man.' I ran home and cried" (in *Edmonton Sunday Sun*, 16).

William Cameron: "[A] shot, sounding as if just outside the building, brought my heart for an instant into my mouth. Two more followed in quick succession.... On the hill before the police barracks which I had quitted only ten minutes before lay the form of a man. It was the lifeless body of poor Quinn. Dust and smoke filled the air; whoops and shrieks and the clatter of galloping hooves blended in a weird and ghastly symphony. High over all swelled the deadly war chant of the Plains Crees, bursting from a hundred sinewy throats. I heard the peculiarly-ringing voice of Wandering Spirit calling on his followers to shoot the other whites and burst after burst sounded the death knell of other of my friends ..." (Cameron, 50–1).

Rudy Wiebe: "Big Bear burst from James Simpson's house, down the knoll straight into the dust and smoke and cries and shooting. He roared: '*Tesqua, tesqua!* Stop! STOP!' but his great voice was lost in the immense lake and creek valley and the far hills.... He was not quite at the place where they were shooting, facing the cloudless sky and his hands were working as if trying to squash down something boiling in front of him" (Wiebe, 259).

Fred Horse: "As soon as [grandfather Kamistatum] heard that first fateful shot, he ran outside in time to see the agent spin around and fall to the ground. He jumped back into the Simpson house, telling the two women to hurry, that the agent had been shot. They could hear Wandering Spirit's distinctive voice calling to the other Indians to kill the white men. Then the terrified Cameron ran into the house and began to plead with Kamistatum for advice. 'Tell me what I should do, they are going to kill me too!' Kamistatum assured Cameron that he would do his best to save him. Kamistatum got a blanket large enough to cover the clerk completely, feet and all. Then, knowing that he was asking quite a lot, he turned to the two women and asked them to take Cameron along with them to the [Cree] campsite.... They knew it could well mean risking their lives but the two women agreed with the plan. They hurried out of the house taking the muffled clerk with them ..." (in Goodwill, 70).

Rudy Wiebe: "Down the slope, walking towards the creek, Delaney lifted his head at the shots but did not look around. 'They're shooting into the air,' he said to his wife, feeling her fingers clench on his arm. 'They haven't had so much fun for quite a while.' Williscraft was running past the Gowanlocks towards the Delaneys. A rifle fired, his cap leaped from his head but he ran only faster, his grey hair streaming in the air, screaming in English, 'Don't shoot! O don't shoot!' He Speaks Our Tongue took him then, very neatly with two fast shots as he ran and his body hit the ground so hard it bounced, still screaming, into the brush" (Wiebe, 259).

Theresa Gowanlock: "On seeing this, I began crying, and my husband tried to comfort me … and immediately an Indian behind us fired, and my husband fell beside me, his arm pulling from mine. I tried to assist him from falling. He put out his arms for me and fell, and I fell down beside him and buried my face on his, while his life was ebbing away so quickly and was prepared for the next shot myself, thinking I was going with him too. But death just then was not ordained for me, I had yet to live" (Gowanlock, 16).

Theresa Delaney: "I felt my husband's arm drop from mine — and he said, 'I am shot too!' Just then the priests rushed up and Father Fafard was saying something in French, which I could not catch. My husband staggered over about two hundred feet from me and then back again and fell down beside me. I bent down and raised his head on my lap. I think over forty shots must have been fired, but I could not tell which side the shot came from that hit my husband. I called Father Fafard, and he came over. He knelt down and asked my husband if he could say the 'confiteor.' My husband said 'yes' and then repeated the prayer end to end. As he finished the prayer, the priest said: 'My poor brother, I think you are safe with God,' and as the words died on his lips he received his death-wound and fell prostrate across my husband. I did not see who fired the shot …" (Delaney, 70).

Father Laurent Legoff, Oblate priest: "When Delaney fell, Father Fafard rushed over to give him absolution, and while leaning over Delaney's body, a bullet fired by Wandering Spirit struck him. The bullet penetrated the neck just below the ear. The unfortunate priest tried to get up. An Indian leaned toward him and urged him not to move for they would think him dead and he might escape. Father Marchand, walking toward the Indian camp, was in front of Father Fafard in the midst of warriors. He turned around at the sound of gunfire and saw Father Fafard fall. He waved his handkerchief and shouted to the white men that they should run for their lives. At the same time he was moving toward Father Fafard, he was hit by a bullet in the corner of the mouth between the nose and left cheek, and was instantly killed" (in Hughes, 299).

George Stanley: "By the time I got there, I found one of the Fathers lying helpless on the ground with blood streaming from his throat. He was still alive, breathing slowly. I said to him, 'I am very sorry for you but it must be God's will.' I took some grass to try to wipe away the blood which was coming from a gash in his throat. This was not very satisfactory, so I took my black silk handkerchief and tied it around his neck.... After I finished working with the Priest and knowing that he was dead, I made for the Agent's house. I had only gone a few steps when I found the Farm Instructor and Father Cree [sic] lying dead on the ground. I began to get frightened and ran on a short distance but returned to the bodies. I made another start for the Agency and had not gone far when I found the manager of the Grist mill dead on the ground. I walked on about ten yards when I heard a step behind me, Cheskwa-Cheskwa. I stopped and waited. It was my uncle Kapechos who had been sent ahead by my father to keep a watch on me. I felt better now as being alone among these dead bodies was not a pleasant feeling.

"Kapechos and I walked over to the Agent's house. Here we found the Agent and the Carpenter lying dead just outside the building.... When we got [to the church], everything was damaged. I saw two kegs of wine that the church had had. I saw the Indians open these kegs and drink of the wine. The rest they poured on the ground. A few of Big Bear's Indians clothed themselves in the Priest's robes. I joined in with them as they were having a good time. I went to the Priest's house and found on the floor a good black hat. I took this and put it on my head" (in Hughes, 162–3).

Fred Horse: "Not long after Kamistatum had headed out, the bodies of the two priests were taken into the church and the Indians set fire to the building. As the black smoke churned upward into the cold blue sky, other fires were started. The once pretty and picturesque little hamlet of Frog Lake was burning to the ground" (in Goodwill, 71).

Margaret Quinney, trapper and elder: "Early on the morning of April 2, the Woods Cree had an intuitive feeling that something was going on. They 'knew there was something weird that was happening. They could tell from the spirits.' Quinney's grandfather [Wood Cree scout Simon Gadwa], his brother and another scout made their way to the tiny settlement of Frog Lake. 'There was a little hill where they stopped and sat and smoked their pipes and prayed,' said Quinney. It was from that hill that they noticed the smoke from the settlement. 'The door to the ration house [the Hudson's Bay Company store] was kicked in when they got there,' Quinney related, and big piles of flour, rice and bacon were strewn everywhere. It was the smoke from the burning church which had caught the trio's eye on the hill, and they were anxious to find out the fate of the priest, Fr Leon Adelard Fafard, whom the Woods Cree held in high esteem, and called Yellow Star.

"One of Big Bear's men, Leaning Pail, rode up to them, and Gadwa demanded to know the whereabouts of the priest. Instructed to look through the door of the flaming church 'they looked in there and they could see the priest burning.'... That night the Plains Cree celebrated their victory and the sudden abundance of food. The bacon from the store house was cooked over willow branches and the Indians donned the robes of the priests and drank from the chalices. Catching sight of Gadwa, Leaning Pail attacked him with a knife, 'but my grandfather took the knife and broke it in his hand'" (in Feutl, 54).

Blair Stonechild and Bill Waiser: "When the old chief [Big Bear] discovered what was taking place early that morning, he hurried to the settlement and chastised the men who were now pillaging the HBC store. Later, he also tried to maintain peace at the church while the two priests performed their Holy Thursday service. And when the situation grew completely out of control, he sent a girl to get help from the Woods Cree at the nearby Kehiwin reserve" (Stonechild & Waiser, 116).

MK: Learning of the trouble at Frog Lake, residents of the reserve of Long Lake (Kehiwin) some fifty kilometres away, some of whom had family in the settlement, left for Frog Lake with their old chief, Kehiwin. Mary Dion, originally of Frog Lake but now married to a Long Lake Cree, described the scene: "The women, children, and old men trailed behind [the men], the majority travelling by pack horse; there were a few carts while others carried their tents and everything they had on their backs. We presented a pitiful caravan" (in Dion, *My Tribe the Crees*, 94).

Mary Dion: "As we neared the settlement we saw smoke where buildings were still burning. When we arrived at the camp, which was across Frog Creek and not far from the lake, the first thing we saw was that a big dance was going on. I noticed that the Plains Crees were wearing various pieces of the priests' vestments. I noted in particular a young man named *Kanipitetew* wearing the long cloak which is commonly used by the priests at evening vespers; another man, *Osasawehaw*, was wearing several strings of prayer beads around his neck. I looked around in dismay for my mother, then left my horse and ran to meet her. I fell into her arms and, burying my face in her breasts I had a good cry. People everywhere were either crying or trying to sing. An old fellow riding around the camp had made up a song of his own and I could not help but catch every word he put into his weird chant, namely: 'Sioux Speaker, will you again shake your head when I plead, a piece of bacon'"(in Dion, 95)?

Blair Stonechild and Bill Waiser: "**In the end, though, Big Bear was helpless to prevent the rounding up of government officials and settlers, especially once the warriors found cases of alcohol-based liquid pain killer and several casks of communion wine during their looting**" (Stonechild & Waiser, 116).

Theresa Gowanlock: "**An Indian came and took me away from my dying husband's side, and I refused to leave. Oh! to think of leaving my dear husband lying there for those cruel Indians to dance around. I begged of the Indian to let me stay with him, but he took my arm and pulled me away. Just before this, I saw Mr. Delaney and a priest fall, and Mrs. Delaney was taken away in the same manner that I was. I [was] still looking back to where my poor husband was lying dead; the Indian motioned to where he was going to take me, and on we went. I thought my heart would break; I would rather have died with my husband and been at rest**" (Gowanlock, 15–6).

Theresa Delaney: "**In a couple of minutes an Indian, from the opposite side, ran up, caught me by the wrist and told me to go with him. I refused, but I saw another Indian shake his head at me** and tell me to go on. He dragged me by force, away. I got one glance — the last — at my poor husband's body and I was taken off. After we had gone a piece, I tried to look back — but the Indian gave me a few shakes pretty roughly and then dragged me through the creek up to my waist in water — then over a path full of thorns and briars and flung me down in his tent" (Delaney, 70).

Theresa Gowanlock: "I was almost crazed with grief.... It all seemed like some horrible dream. I went through it dazed and stunned, with power enough left in my limbs only to follow, as the Indian dragged me after him through coarse brush and sloughs, which wet me and tore my clothes and flesh ..." (in Cameron, 58).

Mel Dagg: "Theresa Gowanlock holds her skirts high above water up to her knees, so cold the current cuts into her legs, numbing them until she can't move. She stands stock still in the middle of the creek, the cold current rushing against her legs. It comes to her now, as if she hears through the shock of the murders, her husband's last words, spoken to her minutes ago, now, for the first time: he was sorry. He has left her alone in the world with his name, left her alone in this, and all he could say was he was sorry. Someone is calling her name. But Theresa Gowanlock cannot move out of the creek. There is nowhere to go. On one side, a field filled with corpses; on the other side, the Indian camp" (Dagg, 82–3).

Rudy Wiebe, interview: "Obviously, white women with their attitudes about how white women should behave in a war zone haven't got much choice, nor much range for their behaviour. Either you rescue them or they become victims. A white woman does not fight.

"And Native men treated them the same way that Delaney had been treating their own women. And this is another touchy point. Just a couple of years ago someone wrote me and said they were going to sue me for the portrayal of Delaney in *The Temptations of Big Bear* as a rapist of Indian women: Delaney would give them food, and the Indian women would sleep with him, to put it mildly. I pointed out there was documentary evidence, and that Hugh Dempsey in his book quotes letters that mentioned Delaney's bad behaviour and that he should be hauled in, but he [Delaney] wasn't even rapped over the knuckles for it.

"So when white men do that to their women, then Native men feel perfectly free to do it to the white women, too. The Indian men were no better in that sense than white men would be. The Indian *women* certainly protected the white women from the predations of the men."

Isabelle Little Bear Johns: "We soon reached the main camp. There, we saw that the tents had been set up in a circle and within the circle the prisoners were made secure. It was very soon after we arrived that we were joined by the leaders of the trouble, those who had killed the whites at the settlement and they wanted to kill the prisoners, thus make a clean sweep while they were at it. It looked very grim for awhile for these prisoners. But it was finally decided that they would live" (in *Edmonton Sunday Sun*, 16).

Theresa Gowanlock (left) and Theresa Delaney
(right). Taken from 1999 edition of *Two Months
in the Camp of Big Bear* (see Works Cited).

FIVE: HOSTAGE IN THE CAMP OF BIG BEAR

MK: Theresa Delaney, Theresa Gowanlock, and William Cameron were taken as hostages to the Crees' camp while the settlement of Frog Lake was turned over to pillage.

Auguste-Henri de Trémaudan: "A regrettable incident — in which the civilized man, out of foolish pride, could not demonstrate an intelligence superior to that of the ignorant Indian who threatened him" (Trémaudan, 317; MK trans.).

Rudy Wiebe, interview: "It's part of the democracy of a Native group, a Native tribe, that even a chief like Big Bear could not control young men when they had determined to do something. When you want to do something, then you do it, and if someone wants to help you, they'll come along. It's an anarchic kind of democracy in that situation: if you can persuade people to do things, then you go ahead and complete your project."

Theresa Gowanlock: "On the 3rd of April Big Bear came into our tent and sitting down beside us told us he was very sorry for what had happened, and cried over it, saying he knew he had so many

71

bad men but had no control over them. He came very often to our tent telling us to 'eat and sleep plenty, they would not treat us like the white man. The white man when he make prisoner of Indian, he starve him and cut his hair off.' He told us he would protect us if the police came. The same day Big Bear's braves paid our tent another visit, they came in and around us with their guns, knives and tomahawks, looking at us so wickedly" (Gowanlock, 19).

Alexander Begg, newspaperman: "Among the prisoners taken by the Indians on this occasion were some French and English Half-Breeds, and these used every exertion to save the women from the deviltry of the Indians. One, named [local interpreter John] Pritchard, in true Indian style, but with the object of saving her, bought Mrs. Gowanlock, giving one of his horses for her, and then he and Nolin purchased Mrs. Delaney for two horses. In this way, these two ladies were saved from worse than death, and placed where they were secure from harm" (Begg, *History*, 209).

William Cameron: "Besides James K. Simpson [factor at Frog Lake] and myself, there were in the camp two white women, the wives of the murdered Gowanlock and Delaney. These unfortunate ladies were dragged from the bodies of their dying husbands by the savages and taken to camp, where they were purchased from their captors by John Pritchard, Quinn's half-breed interpreter, Adolphus Nolin and Pierre Blondin. Pritchard deserves all praise for his unselfish and loyal part, for had the Indians retained possession of the women it is not difficult to divine the fate before them" (Cameron, 58).

Theresa Gowanlock: "I asked to be put with Mrs. Delaney but the Indian, who understood sufficient English to know what I meant, answered no and pushed me into his tent. The squaws inside noticed I was shaking with cold and took off my shoes and dried them and offered me something to eat. Blondin came a little later and bought me for a horse and thirty dollars. I was then permitted to join Mrs. Delaney in Pritchard's tent. Like Mrs. Delaney, I dread to imagine the treatment to which we would have been subjected had it not been for Pritchard" (in Cameron, 60-1).

Theresa Delaney: "I was put into an Indian tent and left there until nightfall, when John Pritchard came and purchased my release with horses, and I believe both Mrs. Gowanlock and myself owe him our escape from terrible treatment and subsequent death.... On four different nights Indians approached our tent, but the determination of Pritchard and some other halfbreeds saved us" (in Cameron, 60).

"I was not allowed outside of the tent, and so had no opportunity of returning to my dead husband, and have never seen him since. At night time, two Half-breeds, John Pritchard and Adolphus Nolan [Nolin] came and purchased our release by giving horses to the Indians, the only two horses they had. These Breeds were prisoners also, so that I was virtually still a prisoner with Big Bear; but John Pritchard and all the Breeds were most kind, and I wish to state that I believe both Mrs. Gowanlock and I owe our escape from terrible treatment, and at last massacre, to John Pritchard and other friendly Breeds, prisoners like ourselves" (in Mulvany, 404).

"Towards evening [of April 2] I went to Johnny Pritchard's tent and asked him to buy me. He said he had been trying all day but could not succeed, however he expected to strike a bargain before night. He had only one horse and the Indians wanted two horses for me. As good luck would have it, he got Nolin — another half-breed — to give the second horse. It was all they had and yet they willingly parted with that *all*, to save me from inhuman treatment, and even worse than a hundred deaths....

"For three weeks I was watched, as a cat would watch a mouse. All night long Indians kept prowling about the tent, coming in, going out, returning; they resembled, at times, a pack of wolves skulking around their prey, and at times they seemed to resemble a herd of demons ..." (Delaney, 70–1).

Mrs. J. Sayers Sr., daughter of John Pritchard: "But [Blondin] really had a lustful eye on the pretty woman [Gowanlock] and tried to talk her into going away from the camp with him. She was not so miserable that she could not see what was on his mind and the poor woman again appealed to Pritchard to help her. The kindly man comforted her immediately. 'Yes, Mrs. Gowanlock, you can share my tent, with myself and family, and I will protect you,' he promised. It meant that he had to guard her from Blondin as well as the animosity of the Indians and as a prisoner himself, it was going to be risky — even riskier than his status as an Indian department employee.

"It was also difficult for his wife. She already had nine children to care for in the confined space of one tent" (in Goodwill, 73).

William Cameron: "For the conduct of those splendid fellows, John Pritchard and Adolphus Nolin who saved the white women from treatment that will not bear dwelling upon, there can be only the warmest admiration.... It is a tale that should endure. That the rescuers were natives and only in part white is all the more to their credit and clear proof that, contrary to what seems a popular impression, a man need not be wholly white to be human" (Cameron, 67–8).

School pupil, class of Annie Long, Grade VII, St-Vital School, Battleford, SK, 1923: "John Pritchard at the massacre at Frog Lake risked his life many times to save two white women whom the Indians captured intending to make them members of their tribe. The two women were Mrs. Darnley [sic] and Mrs. Gowanlock. Mrs. Darnley, the first to be captured, was treated very cruelly at first. It is said that when the Indians were crossing a large body of water they removed their boots and stockings and so Mrs. Darnley had to do the same. The Indians being accustomed to this didn't mind it in the least but the water having ice floating around in it and so bitterly cold that it was all Mrs. Darnley could do to stand it till they were across. When they reached the other side, she sat down by a small fire and tried to warm her frozen feet, this only increased her suffering" (University of Saskatchewan Archives).

Theresa Gowanlock: "On Saturday the day before Easter, we induced some half-breeds to take our husbands' bodies and bury them. They placed them, with those of the priests, under the church. The Indians would not allow the other bodies to be moved. And dreadful to relate, those inhuman wretches set fire to the church, and with yelling and dancing witnessed it burn to the ground. The bodies, I afterwards heard, were charred beyond recognition.

"On Easter Sunday night there was a heavy thunder storm and before morning it turned cold and snowed; the tent pole broke, coming down within an inch of my head, the snow blowing in and our bedding all covered with it and nothing to keep us warm" (Gowanlock, 20).

Prime Minister Sir John A. Macdonald: *Friday, April 10, 1885, in the House of Commons:* "I regret to have to announce to the House ... that there has been a massacre, I may say at Frog Lake, which is a lake forty miles north of Fort Pitt. A telegram has been received from Mr. Dickens, who commands the Mounted Police at Fort Pitt. He says:

"'There was a massacre at Frog Lake — the following were killed: T.T. Quinn, Indian Agent, a half-breed; James Delaney, farm instructor; Mr. Gowanlock and wife; Rev Fr Fafard, a priest, Fr Lemarchand, a priest, and two other men — I believe they were lay brethren. Mrs. Delaney is a prisoner. H. Quinn, nephew of Quinn who was murdered escaped and arrived here yesterday. The fate of Mr. Cameron of the Hudson's Bay Company is unknown. Under Inspector Dickens there is at Fort Pitt twenty-five Mounted Police'" (in Hughes, x).

MK: Immediately after the events at Duck Lake, the Canadian government sprang into action, organizing a military campaign with several components. Major General Frederick Middleton was put in command of the civilian volunteer militias from Ontario, Quebec, and the Northwest. Major General T.B. Strange, a retired army officer who was ranching near Calgary, was called back to duty and put in charge of the Alberta Field Force. Superintendent Samuel B. Steele of the NWMP Mountain Division, promoted to the military rank of major, formed a unit of fifty scouts to work for the Field Force. Eventually, they would all be in pursuit of Big Bear to run him and his warriors to ground.

By April 24, militia units from eastern Canada and some Mounted Police, under the command of Lieutenant-Colonel William Otter, would be at Battleford.

General Frederick Middleton: "Considering the weather, the long distance, the difficult rivers to cross, with inadequate means for so doing, and the fact that the troops engaged were all what may be called untrained citizen soldiers and officers, who had hurriedly left their homes, their offices, their desks, their farms, etc, etc., at the call of duty, I think that the marching connected with this campaign will compare favourably with that of the regular troops of any country" (in Begg, 206).

Nellie McClung, writer and suffragist: "As the winter wore away ... we became more and more agitated by the news that came through from the North West.

"Two women, Mrs. Delaney and Mrs. Gavenlock [sic], were taken prisoners by the Indians and raids had been made on the settlers' horses and cattle. The fate of the women was a shivery subject for conversation. Up to that time the 'trouble' was a vague and abstract state, far away and impersonal, but now the menace had come out into the open, and the evil had assumed shape and image: painted savages, brandishing tomahawks and uttering blood-curdling cries had swarmed around the lonely and defenceless farmhouses, and overpowered these two women and carried them away to the Indian teepees somewhere in the wood, holding them as hostages.

"The newspapers flared with the news; and every inch of print was read and re-read by us....

"My mother stood firmly by her belief that the Indians would not hurt the women. 'Women are safer with Indians than they would be with some white men,' she said, but was talked down by the others, who had terrible tales to tell of atrocities in Minnesota and it seems that most of them had relatives who survived that terrible time.

"At that stage in the conversation I was always sent to bed" (McClung, *Clearing in the West*, 183–4).

W.J. McLean, previously published in *Capturing Women* by Sarah Carter (see Works Cited). (Archives of Manitoba N–13962)

The children of W.J. McLean (Big Bear McLean of the HBC): Top Row (L-R): Helen, Duncan, Kitty, Bill. Centre Row (L-R): Freda, John, Eliza, Angus, Amelia. Bottom Row (L-R): Murray, Lilian, Lawrence, 1895. University of Winnipeg Archives. Western Canada Pictorial Index, Miscellaneous Collection, Image #7924, A0248.

SIX: THE SIEGE OF FORT PITT

MK: In the winter of 1829–30, Chief Factor John Rowand of the Hudson's Bay Company had built a post on the North Saskatchewan, known as Fort Pitt, to trade in buffalo hides, meat, and pemmican with the Cree, Assiniboine, and Blackfoot of the prairies. I read this in English and French on a bronze plaque erected in the grass field near the river landing of the post, described by a visitor in 1859, James Carnegie, Earl of Southesk, as cut out of the woods "within a hundred paces of the river, which is here deep and rapid." Nothing else marks the site, all material evidence of this once-flourishing post having been burned, carried away, or left to rot (it closed in 1890). In 1876, on the rising slope of land behind, now covered by a large farm operation, representatives of the First Nations and the Canadian government had convened in an impressive assembly to negotiate the terms of Treaty Six.

It's important to walk around to the other side of this plaque, for here you read a trilingual text, including Cree, that ties everything together: Treaty Six, which Big Bear, "noted warrior and hunter ... one of the foremost champions of the northern Plains Indians," refused to sign; the Mounted Police sub-post established here in that same year, 1876; and in 1885, twelve days after the killings at Frog Lake, a kind of siege of the fort by Big Bear and a large party of Cree followers who negotiated the withdrawal of the police, took more hostages, and pillaged the fort before withdrawing to the main camp at Frog Lake.

Richard Laurie: "The HBC post at Fort Pitt is said to have been first established in 1831 as a kind of halfway house between Fort Carlton and Fort Edmonton. It was used principally for a place to make pemmican from the flesh of the buffalo that were killed on the prairie south of the Saskatchewan River. Not much fur was found in the neighbourhood except beaver brought down from the north by the Wood Crees. In 1884, when I first saw the collection of houses called Fort Pitt, there was not any sign of a stockade although there must have been one originally as war parties of Blackfoot Indians came as far north as the Saskatchewan to fight with the Plains Crees. The Wood Crees further north were not at all warlike and in 1885 did not take part in murdering the whites although many of them were with the other Indians....

"The houses were of the usual neat log construction with cottage roofs. Some were occupied by the family of W.J. McLean in charge of the HBC store, and others by the Mounted Police under Inspector Francis J. Dickens — son of Charles Dickens, the novelist — who had a detachment of twenty-five men, of whom six had been sent to Frog Lake in 1884. The police post had been established in September, 1883, on account of the threatening attitude of Big Bear's followers" (Laurie, 28–9).

C.P. Mulvany: "The fort consisted of several log buildings arranged in a hollow square and was formerly enclosed by a stockade with bastions on the corners, but as this had been removed some years before, it then lay completely unprotected in the midst of some cultivated fields surrounded by common rail fences" (Mulvany, 117–8).

Heather Devine, interview: "Ethnic identity is based on a number of variables that can shift. That's why in the Northwest you can find individuals allying themselves with others in what we might call communities of interest based on any number of shifting criteria. These could include kinship, and could include their trading or commercial relationships. They might involve diplomacy, religious affiliation, even things like ordinary friendship.

"And this is something I think people don't often acknowledge but there were genuine friendships between Native and non-Natives in this period.

"For example, a friendship which actually transcended the racial differences during the Northwest Rebellion is the relationship of the McLean family with Natives at posts from Fort Qu'Appelle in the south to Île-à-la-Crosse in the north."

Elizabeth McLean, daughter of HBC factor: "My father, W.J. McLean, was sent to take charge of Fort Pitt in October, 1884.... [W]e travelled together to Fort Pitt with horses and covered wagon. We found it a strenuous trip, for cold weather and heavy snow came early that fall. The horses broke through the ice in the creeks, and the wagons stuck in the mud. We reached Fort Pitt on October 29. The winter that followed was long and cold with a great deal of snow....

"It was a lonely and quiet place, so we had to make our own amusements. Fortunately, my father had arranged to have an organ brought along for my mother's benefit. She was very fond of music, as we all were. We would often spend an evening singing and playing together. Sometimes when we had gone through most of the songs we knew I would get my sister Amelia to sing some of the old songs translated into Cree or Saulteaux.... We had two or three visits from Chief Big Bear during the winter. My father always sent him over to our kitchen to have something to eat. Barley soup was his favourite food. I remember his saying, 'Eat all you can while you have a chance. You never know when you may be starving'" (in Hughes, 272).

C.P. Mulvany: "The events in this tragic history now began to tread close upon the heels of one another.... [T]here was, away in the far North-West on the banks of the Great Saskatchewan, far beyond the reach of present assistance, a little band of red-coated prairie troopers, every one of them with as brave a heart as ever beat beneath the scarlet. Their leader was a well-tried soldier whose modest worth, though blazoned by no hireling chroniclers, was well-known to soldier comrades in India, on the rigged mountain slopes of Montana, and in every portion of the North-West, from Fort Pelly to Kootenay, and from Edmonton to Wood Mountain. This was Inspector Francis J. Dickens, son of the famous novelist, and though one of the most modest and retiring officers of the North-West Mounted Police, well-known to be one of its coolest and most intrepid soldiers.... Opposed to them was Big Bear, one of the most war-like and powerful chiefs of the North-West" (Mulvany, 115–7).

Mel Dagg: "'Ah,' sighs the military man with the bright red beard who sits next to Katherine [McLean]'s brother Duncan, 'the Indians.' He must be the Inspector Dickens the girls spoke of. He must be talking to himself, for no one is listening.... 'Frankly, I would have preferred the Cape. I have always had a fondness for elephants. But here I am in Canada, part of a police force protecting the western aborigine from whiskey traders.... Stuck in the Canadian mud!' He slumps forward in his chair and his head bobs in a sleeping nod as he withdraws into mutterings that to him alone make sense. 'There's government for you, Gowanlock,' says McLean....

"'This fall the tension was terrible. The government ordered Indian agents to cut down on rations, and even then, to issue them only to those on reservations. Big Bear hasn't complied and his people are starving. He often comes to the fort searching for what he cannot find. He wants only a fair deal and can't get one, so instead he wanders the countryside, an old man asking questions no one can answer'" (Dagg, 50–1).

Elizabeth McLean: "As the winter wore on, my father realized that there was some unrest among the Indians. They seemed to be very much dissatisfied with the treatment given them by Indian Agent Quinn at Frog Lake. He mentioned this to Captain Dickens, who replied that he didn't think they were any more discontented than usual, and that there was no cause for anxiety" (in Hughes, 283).

Vernon LaChance: "Neither by sign or action did Inspector Dickens show his misgivings. To the people of Fort Pitt he continued to be the silent, slightly gloomy individual of their acquaintance; a man whose seeming habit of introspection was undoubtedly enhanced by his affliction of deafness daily growing more apparent. His familiar slight figure with the distinctive reddish beard was a part of their daily life.

"Fort Pitt, March 1885: on the surface life moved with monotonous regularity. The officers' new quarters were 'mudded,' the buildings and corrals were repaired; riding instruction was given the men, inspection of barracks at regular intervals, reports and returns. The significant incidents of each day were duly recorded in Inspector Dickens' diary" (LaChance, 77–8).

Francis Dickens, NWMP insector: "Wednesday March 4: Todd (halfbreed) trader arrived from Battleford en route to Frog Lake. Wells and Baker (breeds) arrived from Battleford en route to Frog Lake with flour for the Indian Department.

"Thursday March 5: Fine weather. Snow fell during night.

"Sunday March 8: Fine weather. Indians arrived from Island Lake to trade.

"Monday March 9: Mr. Cameron arrived from Frog Lake.

"Monday March 23: Fine weather. Sayers and Nault (halfbreed freighters) arrived from Battleford. Rumours abroad to the effect that the Halfbreeds are in arms against the government.

"Monday March 30: Fine weather. News brought in of engagement or skirmish between the police and the breeds in the vicinity of Carlton [at Duck Lake].

"Friday April 3: Fine weather. Mr. Mann, wife and family arrived from Onion Lake at 1 AM; he reports that Indians at Frog Lake have massacred all the whites" (in LaChance, 79–80).

George Mann, Indian agent: "I left everything and took my family to Fort Pitt in the night. Some of the Indians followed me but could not catch me. I warned the Police, about 25 in number, as to what had happened and they immediately commenced to put the Hudson's Bay Company Fort in order to stand off the Indians if they attacked them.

"We did not see any more of the Indians for some days and as it was getting rather monotonous three Mounted Police went out to see if they could find anything of the Indian camp" (Mann, *Fort Pitt History Unfolding*, 83).

G. Mercer Adam: "Before two weeks in April had passed over, word was brought to the Fort of the approach of Big Bear, Little Poplar and Wandering Spirit, with some ten or twelve lodges of Indians. On the 14th inst., they were descried on an eminence, some eight hundred yards from the post, where they made night hideous with the war-dance, and frightened the garrison by firing stray shots into the Fort, and by scouting round its defenses" (Adam, 311).

W.J. McLean, Fort Pitt HBC factor: "[April 3] We at once commenced to barricade all the windows and doors with sacks of flour, of which there was a large quantity on hand. On the following day we pulled down the buildings which might give shelter and cover for the Indians, and set up a barricade of carts, wagons, cordwood and logs.... As Justice of the Peace for the North West Territories, I swore in every civilian as a special constable, and they all did sentry duty with the police. All were called in at sundown, and the doors were then barricaded until six the next morning. The servants of the HBC, with some members of my own family, and two police, kept sentry duty in my house, which, being two-storied, had the best lookout. Each sentry did duty for two hours and the watchword was exchanged every fifteen minutes. My own three eldest daughters took their places regularly in the watch and proved most vigilant" (in Hughes, 245).

Elizabeth McLean: "We immediately began to work to barricade the windows with sacks of flour, leaving the centre pane of each window for a loop-hole. The men worked very quietly and quickly, for there was the possibility of attack at any moment. We older girls had to hold the lamps and candles to light the way for the men, who finished their task before daybreak. Sentries were posted at different points around the buildings. Then we set up a sort of barricade between the buildings forming the square of the fort, with carts, wagons and cordwood. It was a very poor defence, but the best that we could hurriedly set up at such short notice. The next day every civilian in the fort was sworn in as a special constable by my father, who was a justice of the peace. This included myself and two sisters and a brother ... taking our places regularly in the watch, which lasted two weeks. During this time we practised shooting with our rifles and revolvers. We were constantly on our toes, expecting at any moment that the Indians might come" (in Hughes, 273–4).

Francis Dickens: "Saturday April 4: Fine weather. Extra precautions taken to protect Fort. Johnny Saskatchewan arrived from Battleford with despatch, reports general rising throughout the country. Le Couteau [?] arrived from Onion Lake confirms report of massacre; reports Hudson's Bay Company employees safe, also the women. False alarm at 11:30, another at 4.

"Monday April 13: Fine weather. Constable Loasby, Cowan and Quinn left on a scouting expedition to Frog Lake. A number of Indians arrived from Frog Lake, sent a letter demanding that police lay down their arms and leave the place, they report prisoners safe ... Mr McLean parlayed with them and gave them grub. By contents of letter it appears 250 armed men area around Fort" (in LaChance, 80).

W.J. McLean: "On the 13 of April, Inspector Dickens, for some unexplained reason, insisted on sending out two of his men, Dave Cowan and Clarence Loasby, and one civilian, Henry Quinn, to locate the whereabouts of a large band of Indians. Between three and four o'clock that afternoon, the Indians, fully two hundred and fifty strong, all mounted, made their appearance on the ridge back of the fort. Their first act was to round up the [Hudson's Bay] Company's cattle and shoot seven or eight of them and to make fires and cook several of the freshly killed beef. Later, a note, written by H.A. [sic] Halpin, a prisoner of Big Bear, and signed by the chief himself, was brought to me. It asked for tea, tobacco, and a blanket for Big Bear, as he was very cold. Shortly after, another messenger, an Indian known as Miserable Man, came asking for kettles to make the tea, and for a shirt and trousers for himself, as he was almost nude and shivering. All this he got" (in Hughes, 246).

Heather Devine, interview: "We're dealing with people who have established a number of relationships and one of the things that became apparent to me is that people who are dealing with events as they unfold are concerned about all of these conflicting relationships. They have these ties, these blood ties. They also have these good friendships, some of which are with white people. And they're trying desperately to maintain some sort of equilibrium. All of this, and trying not to get killed."

Sam Steele, NWMP colonel: "On April 13 a large body of Indians appeared on the rising ground to the north of the post. They had with them as prisoners [from Frog Lake] Cameron, Halpin and Dufresne, [clerks] of the Hudson's Bay Company. The latter was sent to the fort with a flag of truce. He brought letters from Mr Halpin, in which he stated that Big Bear demanded the surrender of the arms and ammunition. This offer was, of course, contemptuously refused.... Next morning he sent a demand that the Mounted Police leave the place at once. Dickens refused all overtures and would not permit the Indians to approach the fort" (Steele, *Forty Years*, 218).

W.J. McLean: "Later that evening I got another message saying the Indians wanted to see me, and after consulting with Mr. Dickens, it was decided that I should go with an interpreter.

"On the following day I went out to meet the chiefs. I took no firearms with me to prove that I had no feeling of hostility toward the Indians. They in turn said I had no reason to fear them....

"They said the government had made many promises to them that were not productive of any good, and instead of their conditions improving they were becoming worse every year. Very much excited, Big Bear then said that they had now arrived at the determination to drive the government and the white people out of the country.... Then I told them that the best advice I could give them was for them to return to their reserves and keep quiet there, 'it will be to your good, as I fear and believe you are being misinformed and misled by bad counsel.'... At this stage Wandering Spirit, who had assumed the role of chief warrior, got up and came forward to where I was sitting, then placing his Winchester rifle on his arm, said: 'You have spoken enough.... [Y]ou have said too much about the government, we do not want to hear anything about him.... Look at the few Red Coats (North West Mounted Police) that you are keeping at the fort, is that plenty? Is that all the government can send?... We are not afraid of them. We are going to finish them off before the sun goes down, and we would have killed them long ago were it not for your wife and children'" (in Hughes, 246–8).

Francis Dickens: "Tuesday April 14: Very windy weather. Mr McLean still parlaying with Indians. During parley the three scouts out yesterday rode through the camp. Constable Cowan was shot dead" (in LaChance, 80).

Hugh Dempsey: "The three police scouts, riding back from their patrol, had stumbled into the middle of the Cree camp and were racing forward to the safety of the fort. The Indians, believing the men were the vanguard of a larger force, thought the camp had been flanked and was under attack.... Being the last in the group, most of the fire was directed at [Cowan]. The first man to shoot the policeman was *Koosehat* or *Peesiwoocas*, who brought down both man and horse. Then Louison Mongrain, part Woods Cree and part Iroquois, shot Cowan as he begged for mercy, and Dressy Man finished him off with a blow of his war club. It was significant that two of the men prominently implicated in the shooting of the policemen — Lone Man and Mongrain — had otherwise staunchly defended whites, particularly the prisoners.... The Mounted Police were the symbols of the government that had starved and mistreated them for years. Later on, an army medical officer, viewing Cowan's body where it had fallen, found it had 'two bullet holes in the head, another bullet wound in the thigh, the body ripped open at the chest and the thigh, slashed down to the bone, the head scalped & his heart torn out of his chest'" (Dempsey, 170).

W.J. McLean: "Then Wandering Spirit said, 'You must swear by the spirit that is above and the spirit that is below (pointing at the same time upward and downward) that you will not desert us, and we will spare your life and take care of you.' I reluctantly answered that I would not leave them without their knowledge. He replied that the young braves were excited and wanted to get at the Red Coats, but 'your family stands in the way so we cannot let you go now but you must send a letter to your wife and ask her to come here with your daughters'" (in Hughes, 249).

George Mann: "Then McLean wrote a letter, told his wife and family with all the Hudson's Bay servants to leave the fort and come up to Big Bear's camp and they would be taken care of, for the police to go away and let the Indians have the Fort. The Police thought they would try and go to Battleford, at that time it was very dangerous, as the Indians were on the warpath in that district, also difficult to get down the river on account of the Ice. However, they started, and a sorry looking crowd they were. We all went to Big Bear's camp and immediately were taken possession of by the Indians. They told me not to be afraid, they would not hurt me" (in *Fort Pitt History Unfolding*, 83).

W.J. McLean: "My dear wife — Alas, that I came into camp at all, for God only knows how things will go now. They want you and the children to come into camp and it may be for the best that you should, for heaven only knows how this will end.... For the time being we might be safe with the Indians, but hereafter it is hard to say.... Beyond a doubt the Indians promise that after you all come out, they will go off and give the police time to get away before they come to see the fort again.... We must do all that we can to get out before dark and move out so as to give Captain Dickens a chance to get off with his men" (in "History of the Saskatchewan Uprising 1885," typescript, 68).

Big Bear: "'Fort Pitt, April 14, 1885: My dear Friend [Sergeant Martin NWMP], Since I have met you long ago we have always been good friends, and you have from time to time given me things. That is the reason why I want to speak kindly to you, so please try to get out from Fort Pitt as soon as you can, and tell your captain [Dickens] that I remember him well. For since the Canadian government have had me to starve in this country, he sometimes gave me food. I do not forget the last time I visited Fort Pitt, he gave me a good blanket; that is the reason that I want you all out without any bloodshed; we had a talk, I and my men, before we left camp, and we thought the way we are doing now the best. That is to let you off, if you would go, so try and get away before the afternoon, as the young men are all wild and hard to keep in hand. (Signed) Big Bear. P.S. You asked me to keep the men in camp last night and I did so, so I want you to get off today.' The document in question was written by a white prisoner at the dictation of the old chief" (in Mulvany, 125–6).

Corporal R.B. Sleigh, NWMP: "Big Bear sent down letter. Sent word for everybody to evacuate fort and give up arms. Door barricaded and men in places. Indians had big war dance on hill. Indians skulking through woods in every direction. Mr. McLean of Hudson's Bay Company had parley with them on hill. Double sentries in barracks. Two hundred and forty Indians on war path surround us" (in "History of the Saskatchewan Uprising 1885," *Winnipeg Daily Sun* typescript, University of Saskatchewan Archives).

Reporter, *Winnipeg Daily Sun*: "A demand was then made for the police to give up their arms and be dealt with as Big Bear might see fit. Such a cowardly and treacherous overture was scornfully rejected by Inspector Dickens, who told the messenger that he would hold the fort until the last man was killed. Fearing that the stronghold could not be taken without great loss of life, the Indians agreed to allow the brave garrison to depart" (in "History of the Saskatchewan Uprising," typescript, 42).

Elizabeth McLean: "There seemed to be more confusion than ever in the fort…. What ages it seemed before the police were ready to leave! Their only means of escape was to use the flat boat or scow which my father had had the employees build during our two weeks' barricade. Getting the scow down to the river was slow work.... All this time we anxiously watched from the fort, busying ourselves with our own preparations till we were sure they had reached the river. We continued to watch as we ourselves slowly moved out of the poor old deserted fort. The river was a raging torrent with huge slabs of ice piling up. It was a miracle that they ever got across safely.... The Indians kept firing until they were out of range. We saw them land safely across the river. That was our last view of them as we went over the hill to the camp" (in Hughes, 278–9).

Francis Dickens: "April 14 Indians threatened to burn fort tonight unless police left. After a great deal of danger got to the other side of the river. All the white people and half-breeds in Fort Pitt went to the Indian camp as prisoners" (in LaChance, 81).

Corporal R.B. Sleigh: "April 15: The Hudson's Bay employees, twenty-two in number, gave themselves up to Big Bear. Impossible to hold fort now, so we had to gracefully retire across the river in a scow, and camped for night, not forgetting to bring colors along. Nearly swamped crossing, river being rough and scow leaking badly.... Thus ended the siege of Fort Pitt" (in "History of the Saskatchewan Uprising 1885," typescript, 43A).

C.P. Mulvany: "The story of the engagement is soon told. Big Bear and his overwhelming force approached a comparatively defenceless fort on the 15th of April and summoned the whites to surrender.... Awed by the overwhelming disparity in the relative strength of the opposing parties, Mr. McLean wrote to his family and the other white settlers who were under the protection of the police to surrender themselves to the Indians and come into the Indian camp, as Big Bear contemplated an almost immediate attack on the fort. Yielding to the Hudson Bay officer's persuasion and their own fears, the settlers, unhappily for themselves, deserted the protection of Inspector Dickens and his gallant little band, and left them as they no doubt supposed to a fate similar to that which had overtaken the unfortunate white settlers at Frog Lake.

"Big Bear, however, decided to give the police one chance at least, to save their lives at the cost of their honour and what might have been a surrender most disastrous to the loyal cause. The answer of Inspector Dickens and his handful of Mounted Policemen was in keeping with the character which the force has always maintained. They flatly refused to surrender.

"Big Bear then offered to allow them to escape provided they would leave their own arms and the arms and supplies under their charge to fall into his hands. This they refused to do and the attack was made. The fight while it lasted was a hot one. Constable Cowan was killed, and Lansby [sic] wounded, and for a time it looked as though the police must succumb, but indomitable British pluck and coolness at last prevailed, and the Indians were driven off ... Dickens and his force then ... retreated to the [North Saskatchewan] river.... No more heroic fight or successful defence in the face of overwhelming odds illumines the pages of modern history" (Mulvany, 123–5).

Francis Dickens: "Wednesday April 15: Very cold. Travelled" (in LaChance, 81).

Corporal R.B. Sleigh: "April 16: Up at 4:30 after passing a wretched night, snowing fast and very windy. Moving slow. Several men frostbitten. Clothing frozen on our backs. April 17: started 7 AM Ice running very strong. Had some narrow escapes on ice jams. Camped at 9 for dinner. Resumed trip at noon. April 18: Started at 7 AM Dull and cold, much ice running. April 22. Started at

5:45 AM and reached Battleford at 9 AM Garrison turned out and presented arms. Police band played us into fort. Enthusiastic greeting. Ladies gave us a grand dinner" (in "History of the Saskatchewan Uprising 1885," typescript, 43–4).

W.J. McLean: "We passed a miserable night. It was stormy with a heavy fall of snow, and we tried to keep warm by huddling together in a sitting posture in one of my tents. On the afternoon of the fifteenth I was asked to go down to the fort and take what supply of provisions I wanted for myself and family. This was a ceded privilege for which I expressed gratitude. I could not, however, avail myself of this offer to any extent for my wagons and horses had been stolen. So I accepted some provisions of flour and bacon.

"During the afternoon of the 15th and all day on the 16th the Indians were busy fixing up all the carts and harness and loading them with spoils from the fort. On the 17th the whole motley cavalcade moved on for Frog Lake. Nearly all the captives marched on foot" (in Hughes, 250).

MK: The two groups of prisoner-hostages — one from Frog Lake, the other from Fort Pitt — were now brought together into the camp of Big Bear, still in the vicinity of Frog Lake. Hostages, Plains Cree, and Wood Cree were all living together — about 1000 people — in one large camp run by Wandering Spirit and his warriors.

John G. Donkin: "Fort Pitt, of course, was thoroughly looted, the squaws being foremost in the fight for annexation. Big Bear then moved off into the wild morasses of the North. It is astonishing how his thirty prisoners, many of them tender children, could have been dragged from camp to camp, from April 16th to May 28th, and yet escape outrage and death. This was owing to some Wood Crees who had been forced to join Big Bear, unwillingly. They are very much superior to the Indians of the plains"(Donkin, 141).

Elizabeth McLean: "Just when we were nearing Frog Lake, Stanley Simpson [one of the forty-four civilian hostages from Fort Pitt] called out, 'Look to the left, girls!' But it was too late for me. I had already seen. And what a horrifying sight! It was one of the two priests that had been killed, propped up against a tree in a sitting posture, with a pipe stuck in his mouth. Later on, when my father spoke to the Indians about it and suggested that the bodies of the two priests should be properly buried, they were instead thrown into the cellar of the little church, and the church burned down" (in Hughes, 281).

Reporter, *Saskatchewan Herald*: "On Monday noon two scouts came in from Pitt bringing the melancholy news of its destruction and the probable slaughter of all who were within its walls.

"The story is, that when they arrived opposite the fort at night everything was dark, and that in the morning they saw that it was abandoned and that all the doors and windows in the building were broken....

"The fall of this place is a terrible calamity, as it involves the fate of nearly fifty people; for taking everything into account there is but little hope of their escape or rescue. Even if they did embark on a raft under the safe-conduct of a chief, it by no means follows that they would be allowed to escape with their lives. The opportunity of killing a lot of defenseless people as they ran down the narrow places in the river without endangering themselves is one that perpetrators of the cold blooded atrocities at Frog Lake would not allow to pass" ("Fort Pitt Fallen," *Saskatchewan Herald*, 28 April 1885).

SEVEN: TREK

MK: Now would begin an even more arduous experience: the trek away
from the pursuing militia and scouts but towards a destination
that was not clear, neither to the Cree warriors nor to the rest
of the camp. By now, after taking hostages away from Fort Pitt,
the camp's numbers had swelled significantly. It is difficult to
establish exact figures. The number of Cree warriors besieging
Fort Pitt, for example, ranges between two hundred and two
hundred and fifty, the number of "fire circles" discovered at their
old camps some seventy-three while the number of Indian lodges
counted between 12 and 187 at various times, which included
seventy hostages from Frog Lake and sixty-seven hostages from
Fort Pitt, as well as the residents of Frog Lake. Altogether they
numbered close to a thousand people, now walking, riding, and
carting, from pillar to post.

Elizabeth McLean: "The events of the two weeks we spent in camp near Frog
Lake are not clear to me now. There seemed to be something
going on all the time, but I did not know what it was all about.
The Indians seemed to be holding councils every day, apparently
trying to decide what to do next. We noticed that all these

John Pritchard, 1885.
(Glenbow Archives
NA–1193–3)

97

councils were carried on under the Hudson's Bay Company flag which had been taken at Fort Pitt. All the flags that the chiefs had received from the Dominion Government at 'treaty time' they had destroyed, but the Hudson's Bay Company flag they seemed to prize very much" (in Hughes, 282).

Mel Dagg: "For the first time since December she [Theresa Gowanlock] sees the McLean children. They have their adventure now and revel in it. It never occurs to them that they could all be killed. But she forgets they are a family intact and unlike herself not alone. She sees too that, as Hudson's Bay factor, William McLean and his family are accorded a privileged place in the camp" (Dagg, 95).

W.J. McLean: "On April 19 we reached camp at Frog Lake, where we found [post manager] James K. Simpson and his family, also Mrs. Delaney and Mrs. Gowanlock. These two unfortunate women were in the keeping of [local interpreter] John Pritchard and his family, and he, being reared as a French half-breed, was not harmed by Big Bear's warriors. He extended his sympathy to the two helpless widows whose husbands had been shot by their side..." (in Hughes, 250–1).

Father Laurent Legoff: "On the 26th of April we set out for Big Bear's camp. Nothing could be sadder to watch! The beasts of burden were so thin they could barely support themselves, and most of the people were either weak with sorrow or with sickness and dragged themselves along rather than marched. Many who should have been in bed followed the caravan, wading through freezing water from morning until night. I ask you if that could do them any good? On the first of May, after six days of pain and endless difficulty, the abominable camp finally appeared....

As soon as we were sighted, a few mounted horsemen came to welcome us with their heads adorned with feathers and their faces hideously painted, showing us in their manner that they had social graces. They were riding superb stolen horses which pranced as best they could but which seemed ashamed to have such riders. It was under the escort of such criminal types that we entered the abhorrent camp" (in Hughes, 311).

W.J. McLean: "At this time the Chipewyans of Cold Lake and Beaver River Mission, some fifteen families, with their pastor, Reverend Father Legoff, were reluctantly brought into camp from the Beaver River Mission.... When [Father Legoff] saw me he ran towards me and exclaimed, 'Oh, Mr. McLean, save my life!' The poor father was broken down with grief and fear that he was to suffer the same fate as his colleagues of the Frog Lake Mission. I told him I felt sure no harm would befall him.

"The following Sunday he [Father Legoff] held divine service in the camp, and a large congregation listened attentively. He spoke in the different Indian languages and also in French. The Reverend gentleman prayed most devoutly for good fellowship and Christian love among all men and nations. Strange to say, in the circumstances, a small contribution of money was collected and tendered to the Father at the end of the service, to which the followers of Big Bear contributed the most, some of which they had probably taken sacrilegiously from the bodies of his brethren slain at Frog Lake Mission" (in Hughes, 254).

MK: Meanwhile, on April 20, Major General T.B. Strange, in command of some one thousand men, including the small mounted police scouts under Inspector Sam Steele, started out for Edmonton from Calgary, and from Edmonton eastward down and along the North Saskatchewan River, with the mission to capture Big Bear. A captain in the Winnipeg Light Infantry wrote a friend in Minnesota: "Pray for our being able to get the brutes within reach of our snipers. We ask no more" (in Light, *Footprints in the Dust*, 440). By May 1 they were in Edmonton.

Back at the camp, as the frozen lakes melted in the spring thaw, William Cameron received permission from the Cree to go fishing. This took him and companions back to the ruined settlement of Frog Lake.

William Cameron: "It was a month after the massacre and I had not visited the spot since that terrible day in the beginning of April. And what a change presented itself to me! Where was all the quiet, home-like charm of that beautiful landscape? There were the charred ruins of the buildings. Before what had been Delaney's house lay the head of poor Tom Quinn's little brown-and-white cocker, the dog he had been at such pains to train and whose clever tricks were his pride and delight. Death and desolation now. That was all. Among the ashes of the stables we found the iron parts of some pitchforks and turned back to camp. [We] followed the trail down which Dill, my former partner, and Gilchrist had been chased and overhauled by the Indians on that fatal day, and in a slight hollow rimmed by wooded hills, lying in the middle of the trail, where he had been shot down beside his master, we came across Gilchrist's black-and-white dog. Off to the right in the grass beside the trees lay the bodies of the two men, left unburied by command of the Indians. It was a horrible sight" (Cameron, 114–5).

Sarah Carter, historian: "Those [commentators] who wished to warn against the potential dangers of a pluralistic and more egalitarian nation, and wanted to maintain and strengthen race and gender divisions and hierarchies, cast [Theresa Delaney] and [Theresa] Gowanlock as helpless and vulnerable victims of Aboriginal savagery, and it was this script that emerged triumphant. This version of events was codified in November 1885 through the publication of the separate narratives of the two women in one book entitled *Two Months in the Camp of Big Bear*. In this book their suffering and privation, their helplessness and vulnerability were emphasized, although this was not quite the story that they gave early in June at Fort Pitt. While the women had clearly been through a tremendous ordeal, and an unfamiliar routine, in their first public declarations the women stressed they had coped reasonably well under the circumstances, that they had received considerate treatment, had had plenty to eat, had not been forced either to work or walk, and were very grateful for the care and assistance of some Metis families, especially that of John and Rose Pritchard" (Carter, *Two Months*, viii).

Theresa Gowanlock: "There have appeared so many conflicting statements in the public press regarding my capture and treatment while with the Indians, that it is my bounded duty to give the public a truthful and accurate description of my capture, detention and misfortunes while captive in the camp of Big Bear" (Gowanlock, 3).

G. Mercer Adam: "The captives, for the space of two months, were in hourly fear for their lives. Dragged to and fro over a wild and desolate region, they for a time lived a living death" (Adam, 302).

Theresa Delaney: "Occasionally an Indian, more humane than the rest, would offer a ride to those who were required to walk; and sometimes John Pritchard would increase his already overladen load by taking some weary one up. Pritchard and all the Breeds walked always, though by making us walk they could have ridden ... but they never complained, because they knew their walking enabled us to ride" (in Mulvany, 405).

Mrs. J. Sayers Sr.: "The two helpless white women were not only a danger to the family but an extra burden as well. They were asked to make the daily supply of bannock and do some sewing but they were totally ignorant of camp life and they were far more hindrance than help. Mrs. Pritchard often became exasperated with them: they seemed sullen rather than grateful and apparently resented the assigned work" (in Goodwill, 74).

Sarah Carter, interview: "In the published version of *Two Months in the Camp of Big Bear*, the women claim they were worked to death, that they had to go on long marches on foot in thin shoes, everyone was laughing at them, mocking them; above all, the emphasis is on the fact they were vulnerable white women in the hands of wild savages.

"The Hudson's Bay Company in *Two Months* has become the villain. The company is portrayed as an institution that doesn't want to turn Aboriginal people into peaceful farmers and the Canadian government is placed in a very favourable light as wanting them to become peaceful agriculturalists — and John Delaney is the hero in this regard, as the farm instructor.

"Also, in the published version of *Two Months*, Aboriginal women are particularly vilified, and they serve to define the vulnerability of white women by contrast. They're depicted as performing all sorts of distasteful acts and the kind of manual labour that vulnerable, pure, delicate white women would not attempt to perform."

Mel Dagg: "The men have been gone from the camp for days now. What a relief to be free of their constant stares. The women govern and run the camp, gathering food, firewood, looking after children, tending animals.... She herself [Gowanlock] has been charged with making bannock. She must dig out a hole in the side of the [river]bank and start a fire. She stirs water into the flour and kneads it hard, then flattens the dough and places it in a frying pan, ready to bake. Later she removes the frying pan and studies the result of her first effort, bannock as black as the pan itself. Odd, she thinks, cutting through the burnt crust, for even a moment to believe she could make bread like these Indian women" (Dagg, 9).

MK: On May 4, still camped at Frog Lake, Chief Big Bear received a despatch purportedly from Chief Poundmaker, a disaffected Cree leader from a reserve near Fort Battleford, who asked Big Bear and his followers to join up with his without delay. Poundmaker "would give Big Bear's people a good reception," wrote William McLean in his account, "and for this purpose was holding sixty fat cattle for them." Poundmaker hoped that the joint forces would be able to take Fort Battleford with all its provisions and then march on to join the Métis under Louis Riel on the South Saskatchewan River. But not all the Cree were enthusiastic about the proposal.

W.J. McLean: "We remained in the vicinity of Frog Lake for over two weeks. At this point Mr. James K. Simpson became my confidential interpreter, and was always camped near my tents with his family, as were a number of Indians and half-breeds who were compelled to join the rebellious camp by some of Big Bear's followers.... We carried on our meetings night after night, increasing the number of our adherents until at last we had a ruling majority at the [Indians'] councils. This caused bitter feelings between the Plain Indians who were followers of Big Bear and the Wood Crees, many of whom were very much against taking part in the rebellion [of the Métis]" (in Hughes, 251–2).

Robert Jefferson: "Wood Indians [are] a different type altogether; a people whose experience of fighting was limited to struggles with nature and wild life.... Of war parties, and raids, and horse-stealing, of violence, and battle, and murder, they knew only from tales. With them, the menace of the white man's wrath and retaliation had much greater weight than any problematical results of rebellion" (Jefferson, 135).

Elizabeth McLean: "We were soon on the move again, this time in the direction of Frenchman Butte" (in Hughes, 282).

Joseph Dion, educator: "It is always a difficult task to bring out the vanquished people's own account of any period of history. In this instance, a handful of Crees dared to resist the authority and for awhile these rebels held the upper hand. The main reason for the unrest was that the people were starving and revolt is hunger's follower....

"In the minds of many in [Frog Lake] village, retribution would surely follow, for the whites would certainly seek revenge for the murders of their fellow citizens. There were others who dared to forecast a return of the old life of plenty.

"Regulations governing the old time large camps were revived and put into effect. It was decided to move slowly towards the rising sun, and eventually to join forces with the eastern tribes.

"The store at Fort Pitt would be pillaged on the way, the garrison routed, and a grand time would be had by all. There was nothing to do in the meantime but to dance away and feast on government cattle....

"But the Crees were never ones to take advantage of their conquests, nor were they given to moping, so they feasted and danced for a whole month, all the way to Frenchman Butte, a distance of scarcely 40 miles" (Dion, *My Tribe the Crees*, 97–9).

Theresa Gowanlock: "While we were driving along after breaking up camp, the little fellows [Indian boys] would run along and pick flowers for us, one vying with the other as to who would get the most and the prettiest. They were gifted with a most remarkable memory and a slight was not very soon forgotten, while a kindness held the same place in their memory" (Gowanlock, 32).

Elizabeth McLean: "It was probably during this march that our family began to notice a slight breach between the Wood Crees and the Plain Indians. The latter wanted the whole party to go to Battleford to see what Chief Poundmaker was doing. But to this the Wood Crees did not agree. The breach widened to such an extent that the two tribes were grouping themselves at opposite ends of the camp. The Wood Crees invited us to set up our tent at their end of the camp. This caused indignation among the others, who were however too late to do anything about it....

"It was at about this time that we came to know Wandering Spirit, who often came round our campfire in the evenings and talked to my mother. We noticed that he was quite different in appearance from the other Indians. He was a tall thin man with a long face and a long nose. In contrast with the other Indians, who all had small eyes and straight hair, Wandering Spirit had wonderful large black eyes and jet black hair that hung in ringlets. He was the man who had fired the first shot at the Frog Lake massacre, and apparently he was now very remorseful for what he had done.... We began to notice that his hair was turning grey very fast" (in Hughes, 286–7, 282).

Sarah Carter, interview: "In her narrative, Elizabeth McLean has some interesting things to say about Wandering Spirit. She describes him, not as one of the stock villains of the story, but as a man who was very crippled by remorse and grief over what had happened. She describes his hair was changing from jet black to grey and then white in the course of those weeks. And he was continually anxious to know, according to Elizabeth McLean, how the Christian God was going to punish him. And he was so dejected that Helen McLean, Elizabeth's mother, apparently took him in and he was accepted as one of the members of the camp that the McLeans were in."

Rudy Wiebe, interview: "I see Wandering Spirit as a really tragic figure, because he's trying to live — he's grown up and his entire world is the world that's disappeared, and he can't hold on to it, and he makes one more valiant effort, basically to protect his people. That's the job of the war chief, to protect his people. But, as Big Bear says and the war proved, you need the white man's goods in order to fight him, and he's not going to give them to you. And that's exactly what happens at Frenchman Butte. The Natives run out of ammunition almost immediately and then there's nothing left to do but retreat when the cannon faces them. They have no cannon.

"And, when Wandering Spirit can no longer protect his people as a war chief in the behaviour of a war chief, his occupation is gone. His life is gone, he's got nothing to fight anymore, he's got nothing to do anymore."

MK: On May 14, the forces of Major General Strange left Edmonton — by May 24 they would be installed at what remained of Fort Pitt — closing in on the fleeing Crees and their camp. Among the soldiers rode a surgeon in the general's service. On their way to Fort Pitt, they passed through Frog Lake.

Doctor John P. Pennefather, militia surgeon: "On Sunday the 24th [May] we marched at 3.30, passing by a succession of very pretty lakes and tame surroundings. About 4.30 we arrived at Frog Lake, a charming situation, but recently the scene of a horrible tragedy. Shortly after camping, the scouts reported having found the remains of four bodies. I was directed by the General to inspect them, and about a mile distant, close to the burned mission-house, lay the charred remains of four men. The extremities were burnt off, also the faces and front portions of the head, the backs of the trunks being comparatively uninjured, proving the correctness of the rumour we had heard that, after being shot, the bodies had been covered with petroleum and set on fire. Portions of cassocks adhering to the back showed the remains of three of them to have been the priests in charge of the mission and a lay brother, the fourth being that of the Indian instructor [Delaney]. A few yards off lay the body of a fine young man, supposed to be Gilchrist. The remains were placed in a common grave, and decently covered over.... It was sad to see a place, which had evidently much pains bestowed upon it, rendered waste. A pretty garden, tastefully laid out, surrounded one of the cottages, and in front of the mission was a large, well-tilled field, ready for cropping.... Early next morning I paid a visit to the late Mr. Gowanlock's house, about 2 miles distant from our camp. This proved to be a good log building, beautifully situated on the banks of a small river.... The house had been ransacked throughout, and the paper on the walls slashed into ribbons; a cretonne partition was cut into shreds; the floors littered with books, papers, and letters; not a single article of furniture or even a cooking utensil was left. Outside the same confusion reigned. Around lay the machinery for a first-class sawmill, which would have largely benefited the district. In searching for bodies, I approached the mill dam, and was struck with the countless number of pike swimming about, and thought it not improbable that the villains had ended their hellish work by throwing the bodies into the river, and hence the great number of these fish had congregated. This turned out to be erroneous ..." (Pennefather, *Thirteen Years on the Prairies*, 33–5).

Major General T.B. Strange: "I ... reached Fort Pitt without opposition. I sent scouts in every direction. The [Anglican missionary] Reverend Canon McKay and the [Methodist missionary] Reverend John McDougall crossed the river with scouts; they reported tracks made by white women's feet, and found slippers.... Next day I received information that Major [Samuel] Steele, commanding advanced scouts to the east or north side of the river, had been fired upon about ten miles distant from Fort Pitt.... Meanwhile, I had sent Major Perry with twenty police to reconnoitre south side of the river. I subsequently received a report from Major Steele, that the Indians were in force on his front; the scouts counted one hundred and eighty-seven lodges. I immediately marched with all the troops at my disposal, after leaving a company of the 65th [Carabiniers of Montreal] to fortify and protect what remained of Fort Pitt ..." (in Begg, 238).

MK: The 65th then sailed down the North Saskatchewan River. Mass was held on board their boat on Sunday, May 24. The next day they resumed their journey at 3:30 PM.

Sergeant Charles Daoust: "The evening was rather fine. Toward 1:30 in the morning, the sentry sounded the alarm but we didn't notice anything suspicious in the vicinity. The next day, reveille at 5 o'clock. Before leaving the spot, we raised a cross on the bluff, 40 feet high, to the memory of the Reverend Oblate Fathers who were massacred at Frog Lake a few miles away. The cross bore the following inscription: Raised in memory of the victims of Frog Lake by the 65th battalion. A document relating the facts which had motivated this memorial was written up and all the officers signed it. We enclosed this document in a bottle which we buried at the foot of the cross. Reverend Father Provost spoke a few words to the soldiers, and we concluded the ceremony singing 'O crux ave, spes unica!' We baptised this spot where the cross was raised as Mont-Croix" (Daoust, 81, MK trans.).

Robert Hendriks, author: "The crosses had special historical significance. Soldiers had erected them in anger, provoked by reports of Indian atrocities inflicted upon helpless settlers, in particular two Frog Lake white women, and two priests, the crosses a reminder to the heathens that their wanton acts of savagery would be beaten back by the Christian faith" (Hendricks, http://www.ourheritage.net).

Sergeant Charles Daoust: "The scouts who returned from Frog Lake reported that they found seven bodies, six men and one woman. They were horribly mutilated. That of the woman was particularly terrible to look at. Her head had been severed from her torso, legs and arms were cut, the breasts torn off, and her stomach cut open with the intestines spilling out. They also noticed that all her joints had been dislocated. General Strange, in command of the overland column [infantry], had the victims' remains interred in the modest cemetery of the Mission, among them those of the priests Fafard and Marchand.... This made 18 corpses that were found on this same spot, all victims of Indian barbarity ..." (Daoust, 81–2; MK trans.).

G. Mercer Adam: "For a time, the facts of the tragedy did not transpire, and in the absence of reliable information, as often happens, idle rumour exaggerated the report. The first startling intelligence was of the wholesale massacre of Government Indian Agents of the district, the Farm Instructors and Hudson [sic] Bay officials, with their wives and families, the Priests of the Roman Catholic mission, and the garrison of mounted constabulary at Fort Pitt. A later report still further exaggerated the facts, with the tidings that all of one sex had been butchered, and the other reserved to suffer the nameless horrors of Indian indignity and savage lust" (Adam, 301).

MK: May 26, the 65th Battalion examined the ruins of Fort Pitt:

Sergeant Charles Daoust: "Utter devastation everywhere we looked. Of the five houses which made up the Fort, only two remained. Still-smoking ruins marked the location of the other three. The reports of the scouts served only to excite the impatience of the soldiers finally to encounter the enemy. For example here is what they reported about Mrs Delaney: 'After cruelly abusing her, the Indians stripped her of all clothing, tied her feet together and dislocated her hips. Then all the brutes ravaged her, each taking his turn until she was dead, carrying on until her corpse grew cold.' On another occasion, it was reported that the Hudson's Bay Factor at Fort Pitt, a man named McLean ... was kept prisoner [in Big Bear's camp] as head cook for the band. The two young McLean ladies, aged sixteen and eighteen respectively, wanted to stay with their father. They were given as brides to two of the band's second-in-command. Bride, slave — what's the difference? It was at this moment of the soldiers' rising indignation that a chemise with the initials of one of the McLean ladies was found on the ground. It was torn at the shoulders and spotted with blood. For us all there was not even the shadow of doubt that the girl had been violated" (Daoust, 86–7; MK trans.).

Theresa Delaney: "During our journey we had plenty to eat, cooking it ourselves. Our direction was backwards and forwards to avoid the police catching us. We were taken from Frog Lake towards Pitt, then back again north for about sixty miles. On a Thursday — a week before we escaped — we had a battle, that is the battle with General Strange" (in Mulvany, 405).

EIGHT: BATTLE AT FRENCHMAN BUTTE AND HOSTAGES' ESCAPE

MK: On May 15, the day after Major General Strange left Edmonton, the Indian camp, under the leadership of Wandering Spirit, finally struck tent at Frog Lake and moved down a kilometre from Fort Pitt, where they stopped long enough to replenish their supplies, such as they were, with flour and bacon from the deserted fort. They were moving in the direction of the reserve of Chief Poundmaker, victor of the Battle of Cut Knife Hill against Lieutenant Colonel William Otter and his Grenadiers. Some of the Cree chiefs were hoping to join up with Poundmaker, but, when the camp arrived at Little Red Deer Creek near Frenchman Butte, planning to hold a Thirst Dance on the bluff, came the news that soldiers were on the march from two directions, Fort Battleford and Fort Edmonton, in pursuit of Big Bear.

Struggling along the valley of Little Red Deer Creek, a tributary of the North Saskatchewan River, the militia nevertheless caught up with the Cree on May 26, the same day — unbeknownst to Big Bear's band — when Poundmaker at Fort Battleford was surrendering to General Middleton.

Chief Big Bear and Major General T.B. Strange, Fort Pitt in the background, 1885. (Glenbow Archives NA–1353–16)

113

At the official historic site of the Battle of Frenchman Butte, there is a bit of a campsite now, and a large billboard with a map showing the location of the rifle pits that the Cree warriors dug for themselves, preparing for battle.

Frenchman Butte is, in fact, a prominence south of the site, which I could see rising from the fields and the aspen poplar across the creek. But the billboard reads that, after pillaging Fort Pitt, "several hundred Crees, led by Big Bear, entrenched themselves here late in May 1885. They were followed by Major General T.B. Strange commanding the Alberta Field Force — about 300 men — including units of the Winnipeg Light Infantry, Montreal Voltigeurs, Alberta Mounted Rifles, Steele's Scouts and North-West Mounted Police."

I followed the pathway through the brush to these small depressions in the earth now filled with forest litter and wild rose bushes. But you can see that this was a good place to position yourself with your rifles straight down aimed at the hapless Canadian military forces below this ridge. It is still possible to imagine how the Cree warriors had lain here with a clear view down onto the forces of Major General Thomas "Gunner Jingo" Strange, and rained heavy fire down on the soldiers slogging about in the muskeg at the creek bottom.

And behind them similar pits had been dug by order of Wandering Spirit as protection for the hostages and non-combatants in Big Bear's band: about one thousand individuals. It is mind-boggling to think of these numbers — many children among them — hunkered down in bush and bramble, bullets whizzing past them into the trees. I went back to the billboard: "They all stayed in the trenches overnight.... Major General T. B. Strange and troops engaged the warriors in battle for several hours on May 28, but were forced to return to Fort Pitt for lack of supplies, ammunition and reinforcements. Warriors abandoned the pits as impractical against the 9-pound percussion shells. The battle terminated in a stalemate."

Isabelle Little Bear Johns: "From Fort Pitt we headed across the Saskatchewan River toward a place about five miles north of Frenchman Butte where the leaders decided to call a Sun [Thirst] Dance. While preparations for the Sun Dance were being made, one of the men of our village who had found a spy glass in one of the white men's shacks at Fort Pitt, walked over to a rather high hill and lay down in the grass to search the horizon.... He suddenly detected tiny dots floating down the Saskatchewan. He recognized these as canoes and immediately crawled back down and told the leaders what he had seen. We were quite surprised that the white men had come after us so soon, although we had known they could be coming. Instead of preparing for an attack or trying to hide, we did not stop preparations for our Sun Dance. By that night, the celebration was in full swing and continued all night" (in *Edmonton Sunday Sun*, 18).

Major General T.B. Strange: "On getting Major Steele's report that he had found the enemy, I immediately marched with all available men. Only three days' rations remained. We were already on a reduced scale, officers and men sharing alike. No supplies had reached us since I left Edmonton. The situation was serious, some 300 men, including teamsters, in a wilderness country, and destitute of supplies. I decided to take my three days' rations and attack Big Bear and the Indians, in the hope of making them drop their prisoners....

"It was difficult to maintain connection in the dense bush. The gun, which had to follow the trail, was the only portion of my small army which could not break away from me in this big country. The Voltigeurs, who had dropped down the river parallel to us, left the boats and their uneaten dinners, and advanced with alacrity at the first sound of the firing. We followed the enemy's trail till dark through dense wood, where space could scarcely be found to corral the wagons, which had been brought up. After scouting a short distance in advance, we bivouacked round and inside the corral under arms. The Voltigeurs had neither blankets, greatcoats, nor rations; the Winnipeg Infantry had but short rations to share with them. The fires were extinguished after cooking. The darkness of the night, and the black shadows of the forest rendered objects invisible. The horses were brought into the corral and tied up to the wagons. In the event of attack the men were cautioned against wasting ammunition. Night-firing as a rule is not effective, except on friends" (www.gaslight.mtroyal. ca/revoltx2.htm, 8–9).

Isabelle Little Bear Johns: "Early the next morning ... the soldiers had arrived. Upon realizing the gravity of our situation, knowing that we were going to be punished for what we had done, the chiefs decided to stand and fight. The sun lodge was immediately torn down, all festivities ceased and the women started to drift to the north into the bush. There, the women were well-hidden. A short distance from the site of our recent Sun Dance was the point where our men stood and fought the military" (in *Edmonton Sunday Sun*, 18).

Theresa Gowanlock: "The Indians ordered us to dig pits for our protection. Pritchard and Blondin dug a large one about five feet deep for us, and they piled flour sacks around it as a further protection; but they dug it too deep and there was two or three inches of water at the bottom. They then threw down some brush and we got in, twenty persons in all, with one blanket for Mrs.

Delaney and me. McLean's family had another pit, and his daughters cut down trees to place around it. Mr. Mann and family dug a hole in the side of the hill and crawled into it" (Gowanlock, 30–1).

George Mann: "I can tell you they were very excited, they broke up the Dance, threw off their clothes, wearing only breech cloths with paint and mud on them and rode out to meet the soldiers. Women, children, and prisoners were made to move one camp to a better place of safety and a good place to fight. The women and prisoners dug pits for safety that night. The next morning the cannon commenced to roar and fighting commenced. The cannon frightened the Indians very much" (*Fort Pitt History Unfolding*, 84).

Major General T.B. Strange: "On the morning of the 28th [May] the force was roused at daybreak without bugle, and after a scanty breakfast, again moved forward, scouts on foot extended and flanking each side of the trail.... The whole column was confined by the thick wood to a narrow trail. Suddenly we came to an open space on which numerous trails converged. It was the campground where the braves had held their last sun dance. The poles of the sacred lodge with leafy garlands still hanging from them, showed a batch of young warriors had been lately initiated with the usual rites of self-torture, while the old warriors recounted their achievements in murder and horse-stealing" (www.gaslight.mtroyal.ca/revoltx2.htm, 9).

Sun Dance Song: "*mistik* the pole *nipowiw* is standing *manito* Manito *kanawapimew* looks at him *pi.cim* the sun *niwitcihik* helps me *kitanipowean pi.cim* to stand the sun *niwitcihik* helps me *kita pimohtean* to walk" (in Mandelbaum, 231).

Captain Ernest Chambers, the 65ᵀᴴ Mount Royal Rifles: "With a sort of superstitious unease we gazed at the large Sun Dance lodge, stripped of its cover of hides, which the Indians had no doubt taken with them. It was about forty or fifty feet in diameter, and built of solid poplar tree trunks. The cone-shaped roof rested on a row of strong posts about twenty feet high, and all the pieces were tied together with rawhide thongs. At the peak of the roof hung an enormous ball of cedar (willow?) boughs from which hung, for decoration, a large number of multicoloured cloth streamers. Other similar drapings hung from all the rafters, which gave a gaudy look to the structure.... It was evident the lodge had been abandoned in haste and the tracks of the Indians lead [sic] north" (in Brown, *Steele's Scouts*, 101–2).

Major General T.B. Strange: "On the edge of a wide open valley, right across our line of march, we came upon a fire still alight, an abandoned dough-cake in the ashes. The valley stretched for over a mile in length, and about six hundred yards wide. Along the bottom ran a sluggish creek, widening into a swamp and fringed here and there with willow-brush. The descent into the valley on our side was abrupt — a wooded slope, down which in zigzags ran the trail" (Strange, *Gunner Jingo's Jubilee*, 9).

W.J. McLean: "At early dawn on the 28th of May, General Strange attacked the Indians from the south bank of Red Deer Creek and fought the battle known as the battle of Frenchman Butte.... Before the battle began, we were roughly wakened from a transient rest, and commanded to flee along with the women and children and some old men. We were not given time or chance to pick up any little trinket which we still had retained. Tents and everything we possessed (which was very little then) we had to abandon. We were hustled off on foot in the dawn of the morning, with a heavy dew upon the grass and a dense fog around us.

"The Chippewayans [sic] all deserted that morning with their pastor, the Reverend Father Le Goff [sic], who felt loathe to leave us" (in Hughes, 257).

Major General T.B. Strange: "The crest of the hill was thickly wooded, and the field glasses disclosed what seemed to be long lines of rifle-pits along its edge. They were skilfully concealed, however; even the loose red earth dug out in their construction had been hidden by broken branches of trees stuck in to represent a living growth. There was not a sign or sound of movement; the very streamers drooped in the still morning air.... Steele and his men were close behind, but withdrawn from the brow to escape observation. The ground on our side of the valley was hemmed in with thick bush, which left little room for formation.

"Leaving Steele and his men behind the brow, I rode into the valley with scout Patton. We reached the bottom and were close to the little stream when his horse suddenly sank to the girths. I reined back, and he scrambled with difficulty to solid ground. It was evident we could not cross, so we returned to the crest of the hill without being fired upon. The enemy evidently wished to draw us into an ambuscade and calculated that I would go blundering on with my force.

"Word was passed to bring on the gun, which came up at a gallop, the infantry clearing off the narrow trail and cheering — they thought it meant business. The field-gun was ordered up to open fire, which quickly drew a heavy response. Hardly had the echoes died away when the opposite crest was outlined in a fringe of smoke, followed by the rattle of small arms: the Indian position stood revealed.... As I rode along the ridge, an admirable view of the entire position was gained.

No sooner had my men extended [into the ravine] than the whole line of rifle-pits opened fire from the opposite summit for about a mile. But the fire was without much effect" (in Cameron, 166–8).

George Mann: "[T]he cannon commenced to roar and fighting commenced. The cannon frightened the Indians very much. Big Bear came up amongst the men and women and told them not to be afraid as there were not many soldiers and they would soon kill them and would feed the prisoners on flesh. I can tell you I did not know what to think as I found out I could not get away, as the Indians were watching us closely" (in *Fort Pitt History Unfolding*, 84).

W.J. McLean: "After travelling five or six miles, we halted among a lot of fallen timber. Couriers were running to and from where the fighting was going on, bringing us very exaggerated accounts of how the battle was progressing. About noon, Chief Big Bear came up to us. He told us his men had killed a great many soldiers and some officers. We had to listen to all we were told, and no matter how we felt about the disaster that we were told was befalling our would-be rescuers, we could only be silent.... Eventually we learned that several shells were fired without any results, being fired at too great an elevation and going too far beyond the pits in which the Indians were under cover" (in Hughes, 258).

Major General T.B. Strange: "Meantime, the infantry were trying to cross the swamp: they sank waist deep. I saw the advance checked, and rode along the ridge to the left, and descended to the position occupied by Steele and the Voltigeurs. I saw for myself that it would be impracticable to carry the position by direct assault. I saw that my men were at a great disadvantage, being overlooked by the enemy, who could see almost every man as he lay, while my force could judge of the whereabouts of the Indians only by the smoke of their rifles" (Strange, 9).

Sergeant Charles Daoust: "The General ordered us to walk down in advance into the ravine. Several detonations simultaneously rang out from the Indians' position but not a man of us flinched, not a single bullet found its mark.... It really was an imposing sight! These young soldiers, the flower of Montreal youth, threw themselves with joyful heart against the enemy bullets, which only a Divine hand could deviate from their course.... The first burst of fire was heard at or about 6:30 in the morning; by 9:30 the fusillade had stopped" (Daoust, 90–1; MK trans.).

Private McConnell, letter to a friend: "Fort Pitt, May 29 (one day after the battle).... As I was in yesterday's fight I will try and tell you about it.... We arrived there [18 KM northwest of Fort Pitt] about 2 o'clock, only five or six Indian scouts on the top of a hill, and they got three shots from our big guns, but that was all. I tell you it was queer work going through the bushes and every moment expecting to get a volley from our enemy; but we got none. Finally, we got to the top of the hill that was supposed to be held by the Indians, but they had all decamped. By this time it was getting nearly dark, so a halt was ordered, and we stopped for the night.... In the morning we started on Big Bear's trail about 4 o'clock, I being one of the (big gun) guard. As we neared a deep gulley, some of the enemy were seen going down the opposite side. We fired on them, and as soon as we did about fifty shots came in on us from directly opposite. Immediately the men were formed in a skirmishing line and opened fire on them, and I tell you it was no fun having the bullets whistling in such close proximity to our ears.... The Indians were also under cover in the bushes, and they had rifle pits all along their bank.... The position that the Indians hold is better than any fort in the Northwest Territory. Just fancy, they were on a bank at the bottom of which is a muskeg almost impossible to cross (when no fire is pouring).... It was impossible to get up there yesterday, so we all gave them another volley from our rifles and retired to wait reinforcements.... We expect to attack them again in a week or so, and then we will wipe them out entirely" (in "History of the Saskatchewan Uprising," *Winnipeg Daily Sun*, 1885).

Theresa Delaney: "The women were all left in the woods, but the Indians were entrenched in a ravine, where they had dug rifle pits, as I was informed. This was the first intimation I had of our troops coming. We could plainly hear the firing. We could easily recognize the cannon. The fight began at seven in the morning and lasted until ten. We could not see any of it, but could hear it. At ten, the police, finding they were not strong enough, retreated, and the Indians then fell back into the bush where we were, and from thence back again farther into the bush, all of us having to accompany them" (in Mulvany, 405–6).

George Mann: "The Indians could not stand fire and ran away taking only their ammunition, animals and a little flour and bacon and tea on their backs and at the same time the soldiers thought the Indians were trying to surround them and they retired too" (in *Fort Pitt History Unfolding*, 84).

Major General T.B. Strange: "By this time the enemy had ceased firing. The gun remained in position to cover the retirement. A party of scouts were left to watch the enemy, who did not molest us.

On reaching open ground about six miles distant, the wagons were corralled, the horses left to graze, and the men to cook. Our difficulties were aggravated by the boats of the 65th dropping down the river behind an island for concealment. They could not return against the current. With them went the remainder of our food supply, and the blankets and greatcoats of the 65th. There was nothing for it but to return to Fort Pitt" (Strange, 9).

Theresa Gowanlock: "We fully expected the troops to follow [us] but they did not; and early in the morning we were up and off again. Some of the Indians went back to see how about the troops, and came back with the report that the 'police' (they call all soldiers police) had vanished, they were afraid. When I heard it, I fairly sank, and the slight spark of hope I had, had almost gone out" (Gowanlock, 31).

Lewis R. Ord, volunteer with Alberta Field Force: "I daresay General Strange defeated Big Bear — the enemy was always licked — but why did General Strange retire fourteen miles to Fort Pitt? Strategy, I suppose. He leaves the Indians in their position and then sends word to his commander that he has 'corralled' the Indians. After a bit he concludes that it would be advisable to find out where the Indians are and discovers that the 'degraded and undisciplined savage, you know' has disregarded the courtesy of war, cut a road through the bush east and northeast, eluded the vigilance of the militarist, and may be on his way to the North Pole for all our general knows to the contrary" (Ord, *Reminiscences of a Bungle*, 63).

Jim Thunder, writer: "Now let us go back 100 years to the battle at Frenchman Butte and take a closer look. Historians state that there were hundreds of warriors there and that the Indian rifle pits extended for two miles along the ridge. How can that be? In 1884, the year before the rebellion, the NWMP (North West Mounted Police) took an inventory of the combined camps of Big Bear and Lucky Man during the Treaty payments at Fort Pitt. There were 135 women, 162 boys and 149 girls, and 58 warriors who possessed 15 Winchester rifles and muzzleloaders. Fifty-eight warriors and 35 rifles. It is true that during the rebellion Big Bear's camp was reinforced by warriors from Kehewin, Saddle Lake, Frog Lake and Onion Lake. However, not all the warriors from these bands came, only a few and in small groups. The maximum number of warriors who fought at Frenchman Butte would have been approximately 200 and not all of them had rifles. And those who did have rifles had only a limited amount of ammunition. General Strange's militia consisted of well over 300 men equipped with the most modern rifles of the time and were also backed up with a cannon....

"A monument on the site gives a brief history of the battle. The words on the monument state that the militia 'retired' from the battle. They didn't want to write that the military had retreated" (Thunder, "Battle at Frenchman Butte 1885," 41).

MK: The Cree and their hostages began their retreat north and east toward Loon (Makwa) Lake. Discovering this manoeuvre five days later, Major General Strange sent out Steele's Scouts in pursuit.

William Cameron: "For two more days we travelled, much against our wishes, eastward, living on wild carrots dug by the Indians from the prairie sod, on balls of down — ducklings — just out of the shell, driven by waders in the sloughs ashore and killed with sticks, and on the little flour we had managed to bring with us. We urged our [Chipewyan] Indians to free us so that we might find our way back to the camp of the troops. They refused" (Cameron, 171).

Theresa Delaney: "We kept on moving from Thursday [May 28] until Monday, each day from early morning till late at night, but I had never to walk, nor had Mrs. Gowanlock" (in Mulvany, 406).

William Cameron: "Camp was not moved that day [Sunday, May 31], and we were overjoyed when at a council later, our guards, with no very good grace, consented to let us go. Next morning early [June 1] we were on our way westward.

"A long hard tramp lay ahead of us; we had but one flour bannock for a dozen mouths, yet we stepped out feeling equal to any test of endurance, for at last we were free! — going to meet 'our own people' after this sickening two months of privation, of unrelieved menace, of soul-racking suspense. We must have made nearly forty miles. Late afternoon found us almost under the shadow of Frenchman Butte. We had crossed the streams waist deep in frigid water, but chilled and jaded though we were, [Rev.] Quinney, [François] Dufresne and I left the women with the others in a bluff beside the Little Red Deer and toiled on" (Cameron, 171–2).

Wayne Brown, author: "[Twelve scouts] left Fort Pitt late in the evening and while passing near Frenchman Butte, Sergeant Parker heard faint shouting coming from the direction of the butte itself. They reined in their horses, listened, and shouted back a reply. Out of the trees stumbled three bedraggled men: the vanguard of the captives just released by the Chipewyan Indians" (Brown, 121).

William Cameron: "We walked into a detail of scouts under Major Dale, General Strange's brigade officer.... Our reception was overwhelming…. The scouts dismounted and made us ride, walking beside the horses. The sentries safely passed, at eleven o'clock we were ushered into the presence of General Strange. 'Gunner Jingo' was stretched comfortably under the blankets in his tent, but he sat up and shook our hands warmly while he expressed satisfaction. He had marched five hundred miles to liberate us and he looked his satisfaction at the accomplishment of his purpose" (Cameron, 175).

Wayne Brown: "The group consisted of Reverend and Mrs. Quinney, William Cameron, Henry Halpin, François Dufresne, and several other Métis families. As they got near to the scouts Quinney erupted with the built-up stress of the past months and began weeping openly, clutching Parker's saddle stirrup in relief…. This rescue left only one more group of white captives to be recovered: the McLeans, Mrs. Gowanlock, and Mrs. Delaney" (Brown, 121).

Theresa Delaney: "On Sunday night [May 31] the Indians saw scouts, who they supposed belonged to the police, and they became greatly excited, and in the excitement and heavy fog of Monday morning [June 1] we got away. Our party that escaped consisted of Mrs. Gowanlock, myself, and five Half-breed families, including John Pritchard and Andre Nowe [Nault]….

"We escaped in carts, and the first day did not go more than two or three miles. We went backwards and forwards through the bush, so as to avoid our trail being discovered, and the next day continued our escape, the men cutting roads through the bush, so as to get along with all our outfit" (in Mulvany, 406).

Theresa Gowanlock: "Monday morning May 31 [sic; June 1] was ushered in dark and gloomy, foggy and raining, but it proved to be the happiest day we had spent since the 31ˢᵗ of March.... When the light of day had swallowed up the blackness of the darkness, the first words that greeted my ears was Pritchard saying, 'I am going to watch my chance and get out of the camp of Big Bear.' Oh! What we suffered! Oh! what we endured, during those two long months, as captives among a horde of semi-barbarians.... Some of the Indians it seems had come across General Strange's scouts the night before, and in consequence, all kinds of rumours were afloat among the band. They were all very much frightened, for it looked as if they were about to be surrounded. So a move, and a quick one, was made by them, at an early hour, leaving the half-breeds to follow on. This was now the golden opportunity, and Pritchard grasped it, and with him five other half-breed families fled in an opposite direction, thereby severing our connection with the band nominally led by Big Bear.

"We cut through the woods, making a road, dividing the thick brush, driving across creeks and over logs. On we sped. At one time hanging on by a corner of the bedding in order to keep from falling off the wagon. Another time I fell off the wagon while fording a stream; my back got so sore that I could not walk much. On we went roaming through the forest, not knowing where we were going, until the night of June 3 the cry was made by Mrs. Pritchard with unfeigned disgust, 'that the police were coming.' Mrs. Delaney was making bannock for the next morning's meal, while I with cotton and crochet needle was making trimming for the dresses of Mrs. Pritchard's nine half-breed babies" (Gowanlock, 34).

Theresa Delaney: "The second day after our escape we travelled through a thicker bush and the men were kept busy cutting roads for us. We camped four times to make up for the day before, its fast and tramp. We made a cup of tea and a bannock each time. The third day we got into the open prairie, and about ten in the morning we lost our way. We were for three hours in perplexity.... About one o'clock the sun appeared and by means of it we regained our right course. At four we camped for the night. We found a pretty clump of poplars and there pitched our tents for a good repose. I had just commenced to make a bannock for our tea, when Pritchard ran in and told me that the police were outside and for me to go to them at once" (Delaney, 74).

"We travelled on until Wednesday night [June 3], tending towards Battleford, and on that night we were overtaken by the police scouts, who had got on to our trail and followed it.... On Thursday morning we moved on, reaching Pitt on Friday about ten in the morning ..." (in Mulvany, 406–7).

Mel Dagg: "She [Theresa Gowanlock] is suffering from exposure, feverish, demented. When the soldiers find her she is still sitting on this same rock, trying to tie together strands of unravelled wool that were once her shawl. Her hands tremble so badly she can't complete the knot. Her rescuers, two of General Strange's scouts, are friends of her husband from Battleford but she doesn't recognize them. Arriving at Fort Pitt, her sense of withdrawal and alienation intensifies.... A Reverend Gordon arrives with hats and dresses. A great deal of fuss is being made over her and Theresa Delaney.... People mean well, but she knows they cannot possibly fathom the nature of her experience. She asks herself why this happened but cannot find an answer....

"No longer does she perceive them [the Cree] as she believed them to be, but as they are. She has lived in their lodges, eaten their food. They cared for her and kept her alive. They are a presence, a vital part of the land. Never again will she take these people for granted. When she ponders what has happened, what went wrong, a single word comes to mind: presumption" (in Dagg, 96–7).

Sarah Carter, interview: "There are discrepancies between the version that was published as *Two Months in the Camp of Big Bear*, that appeared in 1885, and their original statements that they made to the press when they first appeared at Fort Pitt in June, some months earlier. In June, at Fort Pitt, they had clearly been through a harrowing experience and their husbands had been murdered before their eyes, but they claimed that they had been reasonably well treated under the circumstances, that they had experienced no hardships or cruelties of any kind, that they had been, in particular, under the protection of a Métis, John Pritchard and his family, and that he, and other Métis men, had been protectors of them."

Sergeant Charles Daoust: "Early in the morning one of the women taken prisoner by Big Bear arrived at our camp. She corroborated the testimony of those prisoners who we welcomed the night before, stating that the prisoners had been comparatively well treated and that the women had not been raped" (Daoust, 95, MK trans.).

Sarah Carter, interview: "They were very specific that they had not been made to walk, to do manual labour of any kind, unless they had volunteered to do it. They claimed that their biggest problem had been boredom, and that they had offered sometimes to do this work of cooking and cleaning. But, again, they stressed they had not been subjected to any indignities or cruelties. Mrs. Gowanlock still retained her jewellery, so their possessions had not all been taken from them."

Theresa Delaney: "I desire to express my thanks to Almighty God that He sent with us throughout such a kind and considerate protector as John Pritchard and the other Breeds who were with him. There is no telling what abuse we might have been subjected to but for their presence.... Four different nights Indians approached our tents, but the determination of our protectors saved us. Terrible as it all was, however, I am grateful that I came through unmolested, and am permitted to return to my home once again unharmed in body and mind" (in Mulvany, 407).

Theresa Gowanlock: "I have heard Mrs Delaney's experience given to you, and I cannot think of anything differing from what she states" (in Mulvany, 408).

Sarah Carter, interview: "Mrs. Delaney had some very sharp things to say about what had caused all of this and she had some very critical things to say about the role of the Canadian government, that had placed her husband John Delaney, farm instructor, in a very precarious position. Yet, when their official version came out, as I've shown in *Two Months in the Camp of Big Bear*, it was a very different version. It was a tale of untold privation and cruelties and sufferings, unrelenting cruelties and sufferings that they had experienced. This conformed to the late nineteenth-century conventions of the 'captivity narrative,' in which they are torn from the warmth of the paternal hearth, thrown into a world of savagery and great cruelty, and experience all kinds of indignities."

Theresa Gowanlock: "*Our* friends were drawing near — too near to be comfortable for the *noble* 'red man,' the murderers of defenceless settlers, the despoilers of happy homes, the polluters of poor women and children. They did all that, and yet they are called the noble 'red man.' It might sound musical in the ears of the poet to write of the virtues of that race, but I consider it a perversion of the real facts. During the time that I was with them I could not see anything noble in them, unless it was that they were *noble* murderers, *noble* cowards, *noble* thieves" (Gowanlock, 28).

Sarah Carter, interview: "The media did play a huge role in eroding and questioning the original story that the two Theresas told at Fort Pitt. It was in the newspapers that you can begin to trace this erosion. The story that they told at Fort Pitt was clearly unpalatable to many who wanted to see Frog Lake and the experiences of the two widows as cruelty and savagery. You see it initially in P.G. Laurie, who was the editor of the *Saskatchewan Herald*. He insisted that it was absolutely not true that they had experienced no indignities; he argued that Big Bear had sold them as he would have horses, that the women were imprisoned for two months, that this was injury and horrible ill treatment. There is also a concerted attack in the press both in western Canada and in Canada at large, on Pritchard, that he couldn't possibly be a hero, that a Métis person at this hour in Canadian history cannot be seen in a heroic light. He was the enemy. His honesty and intentions were questioned in the press, and he was labelled as a 'thief.' In fact, in a letter to the *Toronto Mail*, he defended himself, that, no, he wasn't a thief and that he had protected these women out of the highest interests."

Nellie McClung: "We had a map on the board and followed the troops, under General Middleton, as well as we could; and talked long and loud, and earnestly over the daily reports, before and after school and at noon hour. Piapot, Poundmaker, Big Bear, and Louis David Riel and Gabriel Dumont's pictures were stuck on the wall with molasses, furnished by Thos. James Kennedy's lunch. We dwelt in the midst of alarms, but no one ever enjoyed it more.

"At noon, we played one game and one only. Indians and soldiers. I was an Indian Chief (Poundmaker) and had a red and yellow lap-robe for my blanket. Billy Day led the Free Lances, a force of young bloods who fired on the Indians at all times, even when we — the Indians — were holding a parley with the Government forces led by Bert Ingram who was General Middleton. We had to expect the odd death-tipped arrow from Billy's forces, who did not believe in any other means of communication. No talk, no conferences, no truce, just extermination....

"I made a good Poundmaker, for I had the two long braids of hair, with moccasin laces braided in, and tied at the ends; and as chief I had many opportunities for making speeches....

"I loved making up his speeches about waving grass and running streams, waning moons and setting suns, with plenty of references to the White Queen across the shoreless waters" (McClung, 189–90).

Sarah Carter, interview: "The chivalrous heroes and rescuers of the heroine were the white men from eastern Canada. It could not be men like Pritchard and other Métis. In these ways, the press image began to solidify the sufferings and the privations of these women even before they wrote the version in their book, *Two Months*.

"I think there were pressures on the two Theresas to provide the version they did; and it is clear that they, as widows, had to be very concerned about their future livelihood. They both were concerned about acquiring pensions from the government. And I believe that these kinds of pressures would have been in various ways placed on them to produce this version of events."

Theresa Delaney: "There is no possibility of giving an idea of our sufferings. The physical pains, exposures, dangers, colds, heats, sleepless nights, long marches, scant food, poor raiment, etc. would be bad enough — but we must not lose sight of the mental anguish … and the terror that alternate hope and despair would compel us to undergo. I cannot say which was the worst" (Delaney, 72).

NINE: DENOUEMENT, LOON LAKE

MK: As for those hostages who had not got away, together with the Cree of Big Bear's camp they tramped north through a steady rain, avoiding obvious trail ways. They had abandoned carts, tents, and supplies, and kept doggedly on, knee-deep in marsh, brambles tearing at their clothing, until they emerged near the southwest corner of Loon or Makwa Lake on June 2. There was one more battle — a skirmish, really — to endure, an attack by Inspector Sam Steele and his Scouts at the narrows leading into Loon Lake mid-morning on June 3. It was the last engagement of the Northwest Rebellion. It is known as the Battle of Steele Narrows, or Battle of Loon Lake.

Near Peck Lake, Saskatchewan, on a dirt road that leads to Bronson Lake, you can spot a clearing in the bush, the mouth of an ATV trail, that precisely follows the trail of the hostage-refugees of 1885. They had fled from Frenchman Butte, without food or ammunition for their rifles, bearing infants and the elderly, one foot ahead of the other for five days, wading through swamp and trudging through bush, their boots and shoes falling to pieces, until they emerged here. They skirted around the eastern end of Little Fishing

Sir Samuel Benfield Steele, photo taken between 1900–1903. (Glenbow Archives NA–2382–2)

135

Lake, heading across country for a camp at the first narrows of Loon Lake.

I pull into Steele Narrows Provincial Historic Park. The monument is at the top of a trail uphill. Alfalfa and golden-rod are already blooming in thick profusion and my every step squeezes out swarms of biting ants. I reach the top, which gives me a viewpoint onto the scene of June 3, 1885, its open slopes now covered in very dense bush and aspen. At the inglorious Battle of Steele Narrows, the Cree had been reduced to picking up rocks from the lake shore for their muzzle loaders; they had powder but no bullets, and no velocity. Across the road, in the trees, a marker tells me this is the grave of three who fell — Komenakos, Mestahekpinko, Pwacemocees — "killed in action Battle of Steele Narrows June 3 1885." A white Christian cross is planted on an iron rail, but someone some time ago has tied a red memorial cloth on a nearby bush. Perhaps it is also to remember Chief Seekaskootch (Cut Arm) of the Wood Cree of Onion Lake Reserve, a reluctant participant at best in this short, furious battle. Standing outside his tipi he had shouted, "I will shoot any Indian who shoots a whiteman!," then withdrew into his tipi. He died shortly after, shot in the back of his head when he walked out.

John G. Donkin: "Big Bear with his captives had wandered into the wild and trackless regions beyond the Saskatchewan. Major-General Strange was operating against him from his base at Edmonton, and Major Steele with his mounted police had followed up the wily savage's trail, which was impassable for wheeled transport. This column had engaged the enemy at Frenchman Butte on May 28th.... While the Alberta field-force were scouring the country to the west, an expedition advanced from Fort Pitt to Loon Lake. Colonel Otter was ordered to move to Turtle Lake, and Colonel Irvine marched out of Prince Albert to Green Lake, where the Hudson's Bay post had been plundered. There were about one hundred and fifty mounted police on this expedition. Green Lake is seventy miles north of Carlton. The intervening country consists of dense bush with lovely open glades and beautiful lakes" (Donkin, 154).

Reporter, *Winnipeg Daily Sun:* "The existing maps of the country north of Fort Pitt are very inaccurate, and it is very difficult to follow the movements of the forces under General Middleton, General Strange and Colonel Otter, and Colonel Irvine. They chased Big Bear's band through fearful swamps, muskegs, and woods, over lakes and creeks, the men at times wading up to their necks in water and mud, and being half-devoured by mosquitoes and flies, their clothing being in such a sad state that a correspondent suggested that on their return they enter Winnipeg under the cover of darkness ..." (in "History of Saskatchewan Uprising," typescript, 142).

Elizabeth McLean: "[After the battle at Frenchman Butte] there was much that we had yet to go through before we gained our freedom. When Indian scouts brought word to the camp that the redcoats were approaching, our captors decided to flee with us towards the north. To get away with any speed was not easy, for our way led through rough marshlands. We had to cross little creeks and were sometimes up to our waists in water.... As evening came on it began to rain. When it was time to stop for the night, we were wet through and very tired. My father and Stanley Simpson cut down trees and made a long log fire. We had had nothing to eat all day, but now at least had a little hot tea. We all had to sleep in our soaking wet clothes. I remember throwing myself down with my feet toward the fire and seeing the steam rising from my dress. Before sunrise we were ordered to be on the march again" (in Hughes, 287–8).

W.J. McLean: "From this time our greatest physical hardships began. We were without means of transportation of any kind. We had little or no bedding left by then, and no provisions whatsoever.... Although weak and weary after having no food all day, we halted not to repose but to pass a most anxious and fearful night.... We then started on a long day's journey and were without food until noon, when some of the Wood Cree women brought a small supply of flour and bacon. This very limited supply of provisions we had to use extremely sparingly, as we did not know when or how we were going to get anything again. That night we camped on a fine, park-like ridge between two small lakes known as the Horse Lakes, and remained there two days.... It so happened that General Strange had really won his battle, although he had no knowledge of it.... Owing to a false alarm during the night, the camp at Horse Lakes was broken up in confusion at break of day on 1st of June, and in a heavy rain we travelled all day through swamps and woods in a northerly direction to Loon Lake. That night we camped drenching wet, and had to lie down to rest in that condition.... Before sunrise the next morning we were ordered to be up and marched again, and as we emerged from our tent into the cool air and continued drizzling rain, we were for a moment obscured by an aqueous haze arising from our bodies" (in Hughes, 259–60).

Elizabeth McLean: "That day we came to a muskeg. Ordinarily we would have had to go round it, but the Indians, being in a hurry, decided they could make a short cut by crossing it. They felt sure it was still frozen enough underneath to be safe for us to walk over.... The going was very hard, as the ground was so slippery. Toward the middle of the swamp we saw an ox struggling in a quicksand, and were horrified to see him gradually disappear.... At last we all got across safely, though utterly exhausted.... On the following day [June 2], about noon, we reached the ford of Loon Lake in fine clear weather" (in Hughes, 288).

Major Charles A. Boulton, scout commander: "Now commenced a fresh campaign after Big Bear, for General Middleton was determined not to leave the country until every insurgent tribe had been brought into subjection. General Strange despatched Major Steele, with seventy-five mounted men, upon Big Bear's trail.... The General ordered his mounted men, consisting of fifty Mounted Police, under Colonel Herchmer; forty Intelligence Corps, under Captain Dennis; sixty of my corps; and twenty of Captain Brittlebank's men to advance to General Strange's position.... General Middleton, having now ascertained that Big Bear had escaped to the north, through the forests and muskegs with which that part of the country abounds, this district had to be penetrated ..." (Boulton, *Reminiscences*, 4, 6).

Isabelle Little Bear Johns: "We pushed on our way and finally came to Loon Lake. We no sooner had reached this new place when the soldiers caught up with us again and a battle followed, where many people were killed. This last battle lasted several days and my people soon realized that we were up against powerful odds which we could never hope to defeat" (in *Edmonton Sunday Sun*, 18).

Major General T.B. Strange: "June 6th — Marched and camped at Duck Lake (near Beaver River).... But my infantry were dead beat from marching in rain and through awful mud. The 65th, who had borne the brunt of marching for 500 miles, having been in the first advance, had tramped the soles off their boots — some were literally barefoot, others with muddy, blood-stained rags tied around their feet.... Their commanding officer told me the men could march no more, and wanted to know when they would be allowed to go home. I outwardly thanked that officer for his information, and rode up at once to the battalion. They certainly presented a pitiable spectacle in their tattered uniforms. The misery of their march through swamp and forest had been added to by the mosquitoes and horse flies, which were almost unbearable.

"Addressing the battalion in French, as was my habit, I said: 'Mes enfans [sic], votre commandant m'a dit que vous demandez quand vous pauver [sic] retourner chez vous. Mais, je n'ai qu'une réponse — c'est celle-là de votre ancien [sic] chanson: Malbrook s'en va-t-en guerre-a! Ne sait quand reviendra!'

"It had the desired effect, the weary little French-Canadians shouted: 'Hurra! pour le General! En avant! Toujours en avant!'

"And they stepped out to the refrain of their ancestors" (in Begg, 244–5).

MK: The fleeing Cree bands arrived at the crossing between Makwa Lake and Sanderson Bay on June 2. Once at the ford, they waded across. Most camped for the night about three kilometres north of the crossing. A few Cree set up a small camp on the west side of the ford.

Sam Steele: "When the Indian trail was reported to me I had only 20 of the Mounted Police, 20 of my scouts, and 22 of the Alberta Mounted Rifles available; but, as it was important to rescue the remainder of the captives and capture the Frog Lake murderers, I was directed to follow the hostiles.

"[June 3] From a long ridge we saw before us a large and very beautiful lake with many pretty bays; a long point jutted out from the east side of it, and might be an island; it was densely wooded to the water's edge.... The woods near us being dense the trail could not be seen, but on the side of the lake next the prairie an Indian lodge stood, and in the ford which separated the point or island several Indians were crossing" (Steele, 224–5).

"Two teepees were occupied. The main body were crossing a ford about twelve hundred yards off. I only intended to parlay with them;... they however fired on us, and seeing them retiring to an inaccessible place on an island, the horses were put in cover and the men extended on the brow of the hill. The chief called to his men to go at us. We were very few. The Indians crawled up the hill under cover of brush. The leader was killed by teamster Fielding within ten feet of him. Two more were shot. We then fired a volley into the teepees and at the Indians taking cover, and charged to the bottom under strong fire.... The scouts were on the brow in a few minutes" (http://gaslight.mountroyal.ca).

C.P. Mulvany: "[Steele] executed a clever flank movement, however, and advancing upon the Indians with extraordinary impetuosity, drove them out of their position, causing them to retreat slowly up a thickly wooded hill or butte. After fighting from tree to tree and gradually driving the Indians to the top of the hill, Major Steele ordered a charge, and the seventy gallant fellows drove the three hundred redskins from the top of

the hill, causing them to retreat in considerable disorder ..."
(Mulvany, 398).

Reporter, *Winnipeg Daily Sun:* "Captain Steele, with his police and cowboys, had kept constantly on the trail of Big Bear's band, and on June 2 they came upon them just as the Indians were striking camp, about 9 o'clock in the morning. Captain Steele's force only numbered some 70 men, all told, whilst the Indians numbered at least 250 fighting men, but not withstanding this disparity in numbers the gallant captain at once ordered his men to attack them.... [Steele] took his main body under cover of the bush round to the left, and being unperceived was enabled to open a withering fire at short range upon the enemy before they became aware of his proximity, throwing them into great disorder and panic" (in "History of the Saskatchewan Uprising," typescript, 141).

W.J. McLean: "We camped on a fine arm of the lakes about a mile and a half from the ford. Several of the Indians did not cross the ford that evening, and the next morning they were surprised and attacked by Major Steele and his scouts, about eighty strong. Four of them were shot before they crossed the ford, and among the slain was Chief 'Cut Arm' of the Wood Crees. All the Indians from where I was camped rushed to the assistance of their compatriots, and for about half an hour a hot fusillade was kept up from each side of the ford" (in Hughes, 260).

Brochure: "Upon hearing the shooting, the Cree from the main camp rushed back. They took cover at the height of land on the east side of the narrows and fired on the Scouts. Steele and his Scouts had moved to the top of the hills on the west side and returned fire.

"Three Cree Indians were reportedly killed as they left their tipi. Before the day ended, at least four Cree Indians were killed, including Seekaskootch (Cut Arm), a Wood Cree chief and 3 others — Komenakos, Mestahekpinpiko, and Pwacemoncees.

"The next day, the Cree returned to the west side of the crossing to retrieve and bury their dead. Grief was extensive. Both Cree and hostages alike mourned the loss of Seekaskootch" (Government of Saskatchewan).

Elizabeth McLean: "Quite a skirmish followed, lasting half an hour. Unfortunately for us, five Indians were killed. After the confusion was over, four of the bodies were brought over to the camp for burial. There remained one which had fallen on the other side of the ford, and which could not be recovered.... There was a feeling of suspense that evening as we saw the Indians going out to a nearby ridge, where they were ordered to dig a large grave for the fallen. For us three girls sitting by our campfire, facing the west, they made a tragic picture against the sunset. The occasion seemed even more solemn because of the peaceful surroundings, for it was a beautiful evening. The whole sky was lighted up with the colours of the rainbow, and reflected in the lake, which was still as glass. There were hundreds of loons flying over the lake, giving out their plaintive cries, and as many whitethroats in the woods, keeping up their soft little accompaniment of 'Sweet Canada, Canada, Canada'" (in Hughes, 289).

W.J. McLean: "The scene of the chief's funeral was truly a pitiable one. The men of the tribe evinced much sorrow, and his wife and family were, as is characteristic of the Indians, loud in their lamentations for the dead. Next day [June 4] we had to decamp with the fleeing Indians" (in Hughes, 261).

Brochure: "At the end of the three-hour 'battle,' exhausted and finding no way of advancing upon the Cree, Steele retired to await reinforcements" (Government of Saskatchewan).

Sam Steele: "As there was no sign of General Middleton, not even a scout, and more men would be needed to turn the position by the other side of the lake, I caused a count to be made and found that I had only one day's rations and 15 rounds of ammunition per man. Only two men had been wounded, but their hurts were severe. The worst of the situation was that there was no sign of the support which should have been with me early in the day. No one had been sent to ascertain what had become of the little band of 65 men sent in pursuit of 500 desperate and blood-thirsty Indian braves who held in captivity white men, women, and children" (Steele, 226)!

Lewis R. Ord: "A few miles on we found Steele and his command — that officer not having been able to follow up his advantage from lack of supplies and ammunition — and at once notice the genius and forethought required to make a forced march with due regard for the proprieties. What a vast advantage education confers on a man; here is Steele, a poor ignorant devil of a Canadian, with his seventy men away up in this blawsted, howling wilderness, you know, and no wagons, no tents, no comforts; positively nothing, you know. We come upon a little open patch and see drawn up and waiting for us Major Steele's troop of mounted men, bronzed by sun and wind and toughened by hardship and exposure. Led by a MAN and unencumbered by red tape, they had pushed rapidly after these Indians, fought and beaten them and, after waiting vainly for support for two days, were now ready to show us the way. Truly they are like the scouts one used to read about, and yet, beyond some few lines barely mentioning the fight, I have seen nothing written of this plucky officer and his command" (Ord, 68).

Brochure: "The Cree continued their flight north. They crossed the second narrows, some six km north of the first. To make pursuit difficult, the Cree had chosen an arduous route. They had to cross the narrows on rafts and then wade through a densely-wooded marsh in water up to their armpits" (Government of Saskatchewan).

W.J. McLean: "Immediately on leaving camp we had to cross a deep strait of the lake on rafts, and then traversed a large swamp with dense bush, and water up to our arms, out of which we thought we would never get. Our good ox managed to get through with us, but many of his race were left to die in that dismal swamp.... That night we camped on the north side of Loon Lake, and remained there for a day. It was here the Wood Crees made private arrangements to separate from the Plain Indians. At a meeting called by the Wood Crees, it was suggested that all should go to Batoche to join Riel. The Plain Crees readily concurred, as they were becoming disheartened and tired of wooded country.

"The next morning [June 7] all was a bustle to start.... After travelling a short distance along an arm of the lake, the Plain Indians were so far ahead that the curve prevented their observing the Wood Crees who, instead of following, struck north and travelled as fast as the rough and marshy country would permit. We camped late, very tired and foot sore, our moccasins being totally worn out. That was the only footwear we had. However, we felt relief at being rid of the Plain Indians" (in Hughes, 262).

Elizabeth McLean: "It was wonderful ... to realize that we had left the Plain Crees behind, or so we thought. But just at dusk, the unexpected happened. We saw, coming down the south hill, a sad and dejected figure. It was Wandering Spirit. It will be recalled that his hair when we first knew him was jet black; but now we noticed it was almost white. He walked very slowly toward us, uncertain of his welcome. There was a solemn stillness throughout the camp. One could even hear the crackling of the twigs in the fire. At first not a word was spoken, but my mother broke the spell by exclaiming compassionately, 'Give him a cup of tea, poor fellow!' From then on, Wandering Spirit was accepted as one of our camp" (in Hughes, 291).

Rudy Wiebe, interview: "Wandering Spirit has to be understood in the context of the kind of person he was, and in the kind of society that had already been destroyed. I don't think he knew it. He still wanted to be a war chief at a time when there was no place for a war chief anymore, no place for war anymore, between white and Native. At the end, he realizes he's made a mistake too and that's why he surrenders."

Alexander Begg: "On the 7th June, General Middleton came to a large lake, which was not marked on the maps, and which one of the Half-Breeds told him was named Loon Lake. He afterwards passed another body of water, and on the 8th, found that the trail of the Indians led through a muskeg, which was apparently impassable to the troops. Two or three mounted men managed, with immense difficulty, to get across the muskeg, and found traces of the Indian camp. Some of the old scouts told General Middleton that he might perhaps get across the muskeg with the loss of half his horses and probably some men ... he resolved to return to Fort Pitt" (Begg, 244).

Lewis R. Ord: "We have orders to cross and we turn in for a good night's sleep, confident even to the last that the 'big push' is to be made and that before tomorrow's sunset we shall be squaring accounts with Big Bear. But, alas! once more we have built our hopes on too feeble a foundation and with the morrow comes the musical voice of the aide telling our [Surveyors Corps] that 'the general [Middleton] has sent me to tell you he has made up his mind to return to Fort Pitt.' We are now getting so accustomed to it that we don't swear very much, too sick of the vacillation of our commander to do much but swear mildly at ourselves for expecting anything else. Last night, mind you, the orders were to cross and pursue, but when the captains have retired, each to his particular spruce tree and the general is alone in his tent — the only tent in the camp — the frightful risk of going far away from the Gatlings and wagons, of putting long stretches of forest between himself and his preserve and marmalade jars, of braving the attack of the deadly blackfly and gore-seeking mosquito, of sleeping on the hard ground with his bones cushioned only by his half-dozen blankets and their natural clothing of fat, the awful hazard thus pictured must have been too much for him" (Ord, 82).

W.J. McLean: "We camped late, very tired and foot sore, our moccasins being totally worn out. That was the only footwear we had. However, we felt relief at being rid of the Plain Indians. Next day we continued to travel through rough country with fallen timber and marsh most of the way. The Indians were travelling through the worst sections of the country, to make it harder for any troops that might follow.... When we halted at noon, we had nothing to appease our hunger, and I became alarmed we would perish of starvation. I pleaded with the Indians to allow us captives to go back to Fort Pitt before we were too weak to travel.... They answered, saying they were sorry to see us enduring such misery, but they were afraid to let us go and leave them, as in the event the soldiers came after them, they would have no one to intercede for them, but they had some little provisions yet and would share them as long as they lasted" (in Hughes, 262–3).

Blair Stonechild and Bill Waiser: "The Indians were tired, starving and despondent. But like hunted animals, they had to keep moving to avoid the reach of the soldiers, who they believed would soon be after them. They pushed on across the swift-flowing channel that separated the two lake basins and then plunged into a muskeg that was still frozen in places, yet deep enough to mire several of the oxen. The wading of the 'big swamp,' as Kitty McLean called it, was an act of desperation — a fact driven home by the suicide of Sitting in the Doorway, an old crippled woman who had lost the will to go on and hung herself under a big tree along the north shore of the lake" (Stonechild & Waiser, 187–8).

Major Charles A. Boulton: "At this [north shore] encampment, near the slough, we found a dead squaw who had committed suicide by hanging herself. We were afterwards informed that she was a cripple, and had been left behind by the Indians (as they could not take a cart across the slough), who intended coming back for her with a horse; but feeling lonely and overcome with fear she put an end to herself" (http://wsb.datapro.net/rebellions5).

William Griesbach: "As Major Steele's scouts pressed the pursuit there was evidence that Big Bear's organization was going to pieces. Old Indians and squaws who couldn't keep up were picked up by the scouts. The occasional horse and cart was left behind by the Indians.... It was during this period that some of the scouts from Edmonton saw what looked like an Indian in a blanket sitting up against a tree. They approached cautiously, got into position and opened fire. There was no reply. They then approached still closer and walked forward. They then discovered that the Indian under the tree was an old squaw who had apparently been abandoned by the Indians and had died while sitting under this tree. She had, however, a good head of black hair. The Indians in those days always scalped their enemies and our people were not above doing a bit of scalping too.... This little party which consisted of four or five men were able to make nine scalps out of the old lady's hair, each having a scalp and having three or four over for barter. This may shock some of my readers. *Autres temps, autres moeurs*" (Griesbach, 75).

Lee Elliott, poet: "Bewildered Inn,"

> Perhaps a dream led him from sleep
>
> Down the tree house rope ladder and onto the deck
>
> To tap with his father's screwdriver and a hammer
>
> the name that had come to him
>
> Into a cedar shake
>
> His delicate rhythms
>
> Counterpoint to the seeking of a nearby woodpecker.
>
> It woke me from sleep
>
> Just as the sundance sound of drums across the lake had

Days earlier

Confusing me until I half expected to see the body

Hanging in the tree outside my bedroom window

The crazy woman left behind by Big Bear's people

As they fled General Steele

No one now knows if she killed herself

In hopes she could rid the tribe of just one burden

Or if she was killed

But I think sometimes, when the late afternoon sun

Strokes the thick satin lake

She simply knew better than to leave

And awake alone at night, listening to the loon cry echo

I'm glad for her company

In a few hours the rest of the lake will wake

To this century and engines will churn the waters

Swamping nests along the shore

Radios will drown the persistent white-throated sparrow

Children on dirt bikes will set road dust flying

Lawn mowers will chew

But until then, in this dawn

I'll watch in silence as this son

Crouches over his task

Yesterday's bathing suit hanging loose on his spare hips

Bony tanned shoulders hunched over his work

He carves

The Bewildered Inn.

Isabelle Little Bear Johns: "It was then we decided to turn over the prisoners to the soldiers and retreat toward Big Island Lake" (in *Edmonton Sunday Sun*, 18).

Brochure: "For the 27 hostages from Fort Pitt who hadn't escaped, the ordeal continued until June 24. They travelled with the Wood Cree from Makwa Lake towards Lac des Isles, trekking through marsh and fallen timber to make pursuit more difficult. There was little food to eat, as the Cree did not want to hunt game for fear of giving away their location. They ended their trek after crossing the flooding Beaver River. After giving the hostages extra food, the Wood Cree released them. W.J. McLean was asked to take a message back to the troops indicating that the Cree did not want to fight. It took the hostages four days to retrace their trail to Makwa Lake. On June 23 they met up with soldiers and wagons. The next day they were back in Fort Pitt where the ordeal had started for them 68 days and 400 kms earlier" (Government of Saskatchewan).

Elizabeth McLean: "My brother Willie came running toward the camp, shouting, 'We're free! We're free!' Wandering Spirit, who seemed to have been taken on again as one of the minor chiefs, sent criers through the camp to let everyone know that we captives were free, and to tell them that anything which could be given us would be most acceptable" (in Hughes, 292).

W.J. McLean: "I was then declared free with my family and all the other white prisoners in the camp. Many of the Indians shook hands with me.... Then the chief [Ke-Win, Cree spokesman] took up the pipe of peace, for such it was, that was brought to him with its long and gaudily-decorated stem, and with some tobacco and a small bunch of sweet-smelling grass put it carefully into a parcel and handed it to me, saying: 'I think this is what you want.' I said: 'You have understood me rightly,' and received the pipe with the veneration due it.

"We at once commenced preparations to start away.... Shortly afterwards, [the chief] came to my tent and handed my wife about eight pounds of flour and two pounds of bacon, which was most gratefully received. Some of the women brought moccasins for the children, all with good wishes....

"Feeling grateful at being released after 62 days of captivity, passed in great anxiety and physical hardship ... we then had a journey of at least 140 miles ahead of us before reaching Fort Pitt" (in Hughes, 265–6).

Doctor John P. Pennefather, surgeon with Major General Strange: "Until the 19th of the month there was nothing to disturb the monotony of camp life. On that evening a courier arrived with the welcome intelligence that all the prisoners in Big Bear's hands were on their way to Fort Pitt.... The surrounding hills echoed with the cheers given when this announcement was made to the troops" (Pennefather, *Thirteen Years*, 50).

W.J. McLean: "At 4 AM on the 24th of June we arrived at Fort Pitt, and at once my family went on board the steamer Marquis, where quarters were provided for us.... The scenery surrounding the place was entirely changed since we left, and we could scarcely recognize our former home. During the afternoon the General and many of his officers called on us on board the steamer and extended their congratulations at our safe return. We were also serenaded by the troops from the banks of the river" (in Hughes, 270–1).

Reporter, *Winnipeg Daily Sun:* "At 6 o'clock on the morning of June 22nd 21 white prisoners got into camp at Fort Pitt on transportation sent out to meet them.... They were delighted to see their friends, but were not at all in a doleful state. Everyone was strong and hearty, the McLean girls particularly. Amelia the eldest is plucky enough for a life-guardsman ... and soon after breakfast the adults, children and all were ready for the eager interviewers. Not one of them had been subjected to bodily injury or ill-treatment of any sort. After the fight with Strange they had to walk and pack grub. Miss Amelia says she would not have believed such endurance as all manifested possible, but now that their captivity is over they look at it almost with enjoyment" (in "History of the Saskatchewan Uprising," type-script, 142).

Elizabeth McLean: "For the first time in over two months we had an oppor-tunity to have a decent wash and change of clothing. We hardly recognized ourselves when we all came out clean and properly dressed....

"Months later, when back in Winnipeg, I heard that the remark had been made by one of these officers [at Fort Pitt] that we did not appear to have suffered much from our two months in captivity, for we were all well and our clothes were fresh and clean. It was not easy to disprove this impression, since the whole [army] camp had been asleep when we arrived in our pitifully ragged condition.... It was several months before we came into contact with any of our relatives and discovered to our surprise and amazement that they had been, and still were, in deep mourning, having heard that our whole family had perished at the hands of the Indians" (in Hughes, 295).

Sarah Carter, interview: "There are problems referring to this as a captivity. And this problem becomes particularly clear when you consider the experiences of the McLeans. It seems that W.J. McLean did opt for the protection of the Cree and brought his whole family under the leadership of Big Bear because he felt, at that time, that this was the safest place to be on the plains, at this time of great uncertainty. And it is also clear that there were Cree and Saulteaux who brought missionaries and farm instructors also to Big Bear's camp because they felt that they were doing the best for them, in the interests of their own safety.

"The main narrative from the McLeans' experience is the 1946 and 1947 narration of Elizabeth McLean who published her account in several excerpts in *The Beaver* during those years. So it is written much later than the account of the two Theresas, and it is dramatically different in so many ways. It is not at all the stultified, mannered captivity narrative that you find in *Two Months*. The McLeans had a very different history from the two Theresas. They were from the Northwest in the first place, they were quite accustomed to life, camping, and riding, and they were fluent in Cree and Saulteaux. They'd grown up in Hudson's Bay Company posts, most notably at Fort Qu'Appelle. So their experience was very different. And certainly Elizabeth McLean does not indicate the same kind of indignities and sufferings and privations.

"She also stresses to a much greater degree that there were trusted friends and protectors among the Cree, and she describes with great warmth the assistance that she and her mother and sisters received from the Cree and Métis and Saulteaux women. They do mention that there was some menacing behaviour from time to time but Elizabeth portrays herself and her sisters as being very independent, courageous, not afraid to speak up for themselves. In this way, they portray themselves in quite a different light than the two Theresas who are so frail, so weak, so unable to cope, so prostrated with their grief. Of course, in a sense, they did have very different experiences — the two Theresas had just lost their husbands."

Doctor John P. Pennefather: "With the surrender of the McLean family, and the escape of the other prisoners, and the proven falsity of all the horrible rumours concerning them which had been so industriously circulated, the interest of the campaign died away. Had Big Bear and his band fallen into our hands while these reports were credited, I do not think man, woman, or child would have been spared" (Pennefather, 51).

Frank Oliver, newspaper publisher: "In the events which have occurred lately at Fort Pitt were the elements of a first-class Indian novel of the olden class. There was the hideous massacre, the capture of white women and girls by the perpetrators, and the efforts, at last crowned with success, of the youths of the country at their rescue.

"There is no question that the knowledge that Big Bear was holding in captivity the young girls of the McLean family had a great deal to do with inspiring the enthusiasm which caused the formation of the scout and rifle corps at Calgary, as well as of the 91st and 92nd infantry battalions in Winnipeg. No doubt many a young fellow who joined the forces had in his mind when he took the oath the prospect of being one to rescue these unfortunates from cruel hands, with perhaps a further eye to the result of such enterprises as set forth in the novels....

"But right here the similarity of the cold facts with the ordinary novel ended. Instead of the young ladies rushing promiscuously into the arms of the soldiers ... they took the matter very coolly and seemed — if the scouts are to be believed — to regret rather than otherwise having been compelled, through vulgar scarcity of grub, to sever their connection with their Indian friends. Apparently the bloodthirsty Indians had not been altogether unsusceptible to the charms of their prisoners, and instead of maltreating them, or hanging their gory scalps on the lodge poles, they used them with all possible consideration.... They would be strange creatures if they did not seem somewhat grateful to even Indians who, having them in their power, used them as well as they could, and much better than was hoped for" (*Edmonton Bulletin*, July 18, 1885).

Joseph Dion: "This was a trying moment for my people. The majority of them, though innocent of any rash acts, were nevertheless followers of the war trail; several half-breeds who had taken a prominent part in the battle at Frenchman's [sic] Butte had already pulled out. The Bush Crees immediately set out to scatter for points north. Only the original group from Long Lake, Frog Lake and Onion Lake were left to face the music" (Dion, 103).

Isabelle Little Bear Johns: "After due consideration by my people, we decided to surrender because the odds were indeed against us. When we reached Fort Pitt, after many days of travel... the soldiers then formally arrested all of us except for the very old men.

"We were herded into a compound and guarded night and day until the soldiers started to separate us. Those of us who had nothing to do with the uprising were eventually released while the others were detained…. Within a few days after we were all separated, our men were held in custody and taken east [to Regina] under heavy escort of Red Coats and soldiers…. We others collected our few things and headed for Onion Lake" (in *Edmonton Sunday Sun*, 18).

Joseph Dion: "It was rather a pathetic sight, the surrender, when one by one the warriors who had terrorized the country gave up their weapons; there was a pitiful assortment of firearms of every description, some tied with cord to prevent them from falling to pieces. Then the Great White Leader [General Middleton] who conquered the 'terrible red skins' jumped on top of this little pile of shooting irons and gave them several vicious kicks" (Dion, 104).

Joseph Howard, author: "When they came in to surrender at Fort Pitt, Wandering Spirit was with them. After he had erected his lodge on the field before the fort that night and had eaten his evening meal, the war chief thrust back the tipi flap and strode to the center of the camp. He raised his voice in a song to command attention, then he cried out: 'All who wish to look on me once more, come now!'

"*L'Esprit Errant* returned to his tipi and sat staring into his fire. Curious neighbours passed in front of the lodge and peeked inside, but none entered. He was not one of their chiefs; and the Woods Cree, less bloodthirsty than their cousins of the plains, had never approved of him anyway.

"After half an hour of this, the war chief leaped suddenly to his feet, drew his knife, and thrust it deeply into his side. The blow missed his heart but injured a lung and he fell, bleeding profusely. The other Indians set up an outcry and he was removed to the fort, where his wound was dressed. This saved him to be hanged" (Howard, *Strange Empire*, 498).

MK: Meanwhile, the band of Plains Cree who had determined to reach Batoche gradually dwindled as members slipped away to surrender at Turtle Lake and Battleford. Some one hundred, together with Imasees, fled south into Montana. A handful with Big Bear made for Fort Carlton.

Major Charles A. Boulton: "Big Bear, finding that he was pursued on all sides by troops, turned south between Colonel Otter and Colonel Irvine's men and crossed the Saskatchewan a little west of Fort Carlton. There he camped in the settlements in the neighbourhood, and reported himself to the Hudson's Bay officer at Fort Carlton, and eventually gave himself up.... The news of this was telegraphed at once to General Middleton, who was now enabled to announce to the Government, while Parliament was still in session, that the campaign was over, resulting in the complete occupation of the country and the surrender of all the insurgent tribes" (Boulton, 8).

John G. Donkin: "Big Bear was in a pitiable condition of filth and hunger. He was given a good scrubbing in a tub at the barracks, though this was anything but pleasing to him. A new blanket and a pair of trousers were procured him from the Hudson Bay store. His arms consisted of a Winchester, and he stated that his only food, for eleven days, had been what he was enabled to secure in the woods. A cell was placed at the disposal of himself and staff in the guard-room, and his skinny ankles were adorned with shackles. A little shrivelled-up piece of humanity he was, his cunning face seamed and wrinkled like crumpled parchment" (Donkin, 156).

Justice Hugh Richardson, Regina trial judge: "Big Bear, have you anything to say before sentence is passed upon you?"

Big Bear (in Cree): "I think I should have *something* to say, about the occurrences which brought me here in chains! I knew little of the killing at Frog Lake beyond hearing the shots fired. When any wrong was brewing I did my best to stop it in the beginning. The turbulent ones of the band got beyond my control and shed the blood of those I would have protected. I was away from Frog Lake a part of the winter, hunting and fishing, and the rebellion had commenced before I got back. When white men were few in the country, I gave them the hand of brotherhood. I am sorry so few are here who can witness for my friendly acts.

"Can anyone stand up and say that I ordered the death of a priest or an agent? You think I encouraged my people to take part in the trouble. I did not. I advised them against it. I felt sorry when they killed those men at Frog Lake, but the truth is when news of the fight at Duck Lake reached us my band ignored my authority and despised me because I did not side with the half-breeds.... At present I am dead to my people.... The North-West belonged to me, but I perhaps will not live to see it again.... I am old and ugly, but I have tried to do good. Pity the children of my tribe!... How! Aquisanee — I have spoken!" (in Cameron, 197–9)

Rudy Wiebe, interview: "There's a great range of opinion possible. My view is that, when Big Bear makes that speech and says 'They [white men] can drag into this country anything they want to' — and they did, they brought the big cannon — while the Cree have a few buffalo guns to oppose them — then you do not fight a war in a hopeless situation: you negotiate. And what the Métis were doing was in a sense wrong-headed, as far as Big Bear was concerned. Whether this was the position of all the Cree or all the Native people, I don't know."

Heather Devine, interview: "It's been fashionable in recent years to refer to the 1885 Northwest Rebellion as the Riel Resistance of 1885. I think this does a disservice to Louis Riel, because he knew that he was rebelling against the Canadian government. It was a well-known fact that the Canadian government was in control of the West at the time. The problem was that the government was not living up to its commitments as a government. And, in fact, prior to the rebellion breaking out, Louis Riel had sent messages to Ottawa to try to settle the grievances of the people of the West.

"They were ignored, and, in fact, the response of the federal government was to beef up the police presence in the Northwest. At that point Louis Riel in his correspondence, which we have, begins to talk about taking up arms — but only until then. But, in fact, he is well aware of what he is doing.

"So, to say it was simply a 'resistance' in a way minimizes the gravity of the situation. And, in a way, it sort of cheapens his memory because he knew the risks involved, that's why his fate is so important, because he could have gotten away, he didn't need to commit himself to this road, but he took it."

Isabelle Little Bear Johns: "There were very few men left, only very old ones, but many women; therefore the brunt of the heavy loads fell on the shoulders of the women and young people. When we arrived at Onion Lake, our guns, ammunition, axes and knives were confiscated by the Red Coats. It was soon after this that we felt extremely hard times. With no arms or knives with which to hunt or even horses on which to pack our belongings (our horses had also been confiscated) we tried to move from place to place but found no suitable home to derive a living. The only way we could earn something with which to buy food and supplies was by chopping wood.... I was a strong girl and so took on my share of the job. I chopped many cords of wood" (in *Edmonton Sunday Sun*, 18).

TIME AND PLACE History -- Geography VISUAL TEACHING

CANADA

"BIRTH OF THE WEST"

History Teaching Pictures

The Art League
EDMONTON

Design, Title, Picture and Matter Copyrighted by ERNEST BROWN

Published by The Art League Publishing Co., 10131 Jasper Avenue, Edmonton, Alberta, Canada.

RIEL REBBELLION SERIES X

No. 5014

WANDERING SPIRIT
Frog Lake Massacre 1885.

1885   WANDERING SPIRIT
FROG LAKE MASSACRE

TEN: HANGINGS AT FORT BATTLEFORD

MK: Within the reconstructed log stockade and bastions of Battleford National Historic Site, only five original buildings remain standing of what had been a NWMP post established in 1876, the same year that Battleford was designated capital of the newly formed North-West Territories (the capital was soon moved to Regina) and Treaty Six was negotiated and signed with the Cree. As a police post, Fort Battleford had been a crucial site of events during the tumultuous and violent year of 1885, including the Battle of Cut Knife Hill, the "siege" of the town by desperate Indians, and the mass hanging of six Cree and two Assiniboine warriors found guilty of the murders at Frog Lake and the Battleford area, respectively.

The wind is unrelenting and sets the flag flapping wildly on its pole.

Plains Cree war chief Wandering Spirit (Kapapamahchakwew) as depicted in 1885, in an image owned by Ernest Brown and published in *Birth of the West* by The Art League of Edmonton. (Provincial Archives of Alberta B1716)

A short walk away from the fort along the high bank of the Battle River, just before its convergence with the North Saskatchewan, brings the visitor to the site of the mass grave of the hanged men. A text has been erected there:

"Prior to the 1885 North-West Rebellion, failure of the Canadian government to fulfill treaty obligations resulted in starvation, disease and death among the Indians. Their traditional means of self-support disappeared with the sale of their lands. At Frog Lake and Battleford, some Indians took up arms during the Rebellion against the wishes of their leaders. Those Indians faced trial and jail or sentence of death. Others fled to the United States. For deaths at Frog Lake, Wandering Spirit pleaded guilty to the murder of Indian Agent Tom Quinn. Pleading not guilty were Bad Arrow and Miserable Man for killing carpenter Charles Gouin, Round The Sky for killing Father Adelard Fafard and Little Bear and Iron Body for killing trader George Dill. For deaths in the Battleford area, Itka was charged with the murder of farm instructor James Payne and Man Without Blood for the murder of farmer Bernie Tremont.

"After a short trial, and without legal counsel, Judge Rouleau sentenced all to hang. On the morning of November 27, 1885, the sentences were carried out and the bodies placed in a common grave at this site."

Under a big blue September sky, the reconstructed gravesite is deeply impressive. A black granite gravestone is surmounted by a circle of naked poplar logs, the ribs of a tipi, and is inscribed with the names of the interred in English and in Cree: Wandering Spirit (Kapapamahchakwew), Round the Sky (Paypamakeesit), Bad Arrow (Manachoos), Miserable Man (Kittimakegin), Iron Body (Nabpace), Little Bear (Apaschiskoos), Crooked Leg (Itka), and Man Without Blood (Waywahnitch).

Saskatchewan Herald, MAY 25, 1885: "Good and loyal Indians are among the things of the past."

Blair Stonechild, interview: "The *Saskatchewan Herald*, based in Battleford, had written an editorial in which they urged the stiffest, most severe punishment against the Indians, saying 'the only good Indian is a dead Indian.' That's an actual quotation from the editorial. The court didn't even bother hiring lawyers to protect the defendants. Nor was the translation at all effective. As an indication, the defendants were all given numbers instead of being called by their names."

Judge Charles Rouleau, Battleford trial judge: "Wandering Spirit, you have confessed to one of the most heinous crimes a man can commit. I need not say much, for you now realize the gravity of your offence. You were doing murder while others burned houses and committed other crimes. You could not expect any good to follow your acts. You were too weak to oppose the whites and could not have provided for yourself even if you had killed them all, and now you would starve unless the government took you in charge. If the whites had done as you did, they would have killed all the Indians, but they took the most guilty ones — those who took a prominent part in the crime — and are feeding the rest.

"Instead of listening to wise men, you preferred to listen to bad men as poor as yourselves, you only got in trouble. The government does not wish to destroy the Indians. They wish to help them live like white men, but as far as murderers are concerned, the government has no pity. If a white man murders an Indian, he must hang, and so must an Indian if he kills a white man.

"The sentence of the court is that you, Wandering Spirit, be taken to the guardroom of the Mounted Police barracks and there confined until the 27th of November next; thence to the place of execution and hanged by the neck until you are dead ..." (in Fryer, *Frog Lake Massacre*, 35).

Blair Stonechild, interview: "It's very clear in the case of these eight men that Sir John A. Macdonald as prime minister and head of Indian Affairs, and Hayter Reed the assistant Indian commissioner and the real hardliner, had an agreement before the trial started that they were not going to charge or convict on rebellion-related charges, but rather would charge them outright with murder, which would automatically conclude in hanging them.

"There's a quotation from Sir John A. Macdonald to parliament in which he says that the 'executions ought to convince the Red Man that the White Man governs.' He referred to it as 'ocular proof,' because representatives of three or four bands were brought in to witness the hangings. So clearly the trials had less to do with justice than they had to do with what you might call a 'show trial.' A very strong message was to be sent to First Nations."

Walter Hildebrandt: "Indians called him [Hayter Reed] 'Iron Heart' (it was said he liked that)

- name perfect for him [...]

- subordinates hated him

- superiors admired him

- saved gov't money

- wanted Indians to witness hanging of eight Indians in 1885 at Battleford

- he was quoted as saying: '*I am desirous of having Indians witness it — So sound threshing having been given them I think a sight of this sort would cause them to meditate for many days*'" ("Marginal Notes," *Sightings*, 40–1).

NWMP Fort Battleford Post Journal 1885: "**Saturday November 21st: Morning —**

soft and pleasant. Drizzling rain during the PM… Erection of scaffold for execution of 10 Indians on the 27th inst. Commenced today by Deputy Sheriff.

"Sunday November 22nd: Morning soft and pleasant…. Stoney Jack had up on charge of loitering and prowling suspiciously around the fort and ordered to his reserve. Extra pickets mounted as it is rumoured Indians intend to fire our hay stack as revenge for hanging Indians.

"Tuesday November 24th: Morning dull, cold and damp…. Men busy at new buildings…. Men busy at scaffold and magazine. Drawing near to day of execution of the 8 Indians condemned to die — 2 more days.

"Wednesday November 25th: Morning dull, dark and damp — blowing hard…. Scaffold finished — will be tested tomorrow…. Deputy Sheriff Gibson arrived from Regina on order to assist Deputy Sheriff Forget with executions on the 27th. Number of strange Indians in town. Reported that Sioux Indians leaving P[rince] Albert district — and coming this direction on north side Saskatchewan River…. Number of teepees appearing around town suppose Indians prompted by curiosity coming in to witness execution.

"Thursday November 26th: Weather still dull and damp — ground soft and muddy…. Sheriff's men testing scaffold by dropping at same time 8 bags of bacon 200 pounds each stood test all right…. Reverend Fathers Bigonesse and Cochin preparing Indians for their doom tomorrow morning. All arrangements made for executions…. Relations of condemned prisoners visiting them during day."

William Cameron: "It was the afternoon of November 26th. The murderers had been removed to cells in the guardroom. Wandering Spirit had maintained a stoic silence regarding the massacre and the motives which prompted him to commence it — a silence unbroken even when, after pleading guilty, he had been given the opportunity to speak before sentence was pronounced. My interest in the wild, impulsive man continued acute to the last.... Could he be induced to talk, to unbosom himself to me, before the morrow stilled the beatings of his turbulent heart and sealed forever in this world the thin, cruel lips? I could see.

"I got from Major Crozier, commanding the mounted police at Battleford, an order authorizing me to visit and talk with the murderers. I was shown into the cell occupied by the war chief. He sat on the floor, a heavy ball chained to his ankle. He shook hands with me as I took a seat opposite him. 'Kah-pay-pamah-chak-wayo,' I said, 'you have been shut up here for 4 months. You might at any time have made a statement about the massacre. You have not done so. Your followers all place the blame for what occurred on you. I do not believe you are quite so bad as they make you out; therefore, I have come to see you. Tomorrow will be too late. If you wish to speak, to say anything in your own defence, I shall be glad to take it down. It will be printed.'... He was silent for a long time....

"'[Riel] asked us to join him in wiping out all Canadians. The government had treated him badly. He would demand much money from them. If they did not give, he would spill blood, plenty Canadian blood. Last fall Riel sent word to us that when the leaves came out the half-breeds would rise and kill all the whites. The Long Knives (Americans) would come. They would buy the land, pay the Indians plenty money for it, afterwards trade with them. All the tribes who wished to benefit must rise, too, and help to rid the country of Canadians.... Imasees told me at a dance one night before the outbreak that he depended on me to do this thing. I fought against it.… Kap-wa-tamut, the Indian agent, would give me no provisions. It seemed it was to be — I was singled out to do it.… Tell the Crees from me never to do it again as they did this spring — never to do as I did. Tell my daughter I died in the white man's religion, too. I am not thinking much about what is going to happen tomorrow. I am thinking about what the priest says to me'" (Cameron, 205–7).

Bill Gallaher, author: "It had begun with the buffalo, thousands of them, gracing the plains, there to provide sustenance for his people. Snow lay on the ground and in a thicket a recently constructed pound stood ready to receive the animals. Instinctively, he knew where the herd was and rode right to it with another hunter. They circled around behind the animals and stampeded them toward the pound, 'Yei! Yei!' he yelled to keep them moving. If they changed direction, other hunters jumped up and fired their rifles into the air, shouting 'O-oh-whi!' and kept them on track to the pound.

"'The powdery snow rose like white dust in the sky,' Wandering Spirit said, seemingly lost in recalling the dream. 'The earth shook as if the Great Spirit himself was angry.' The thundering hooves, even muffled by snow, made a magnificent sound, 'the sound of life for my people'" (Gallaher, *The Frog Lake Massacre*, 233–4).

Constable C. Whitehead, NWMP, on duty: "This was a public execution. The scaffold was erected in the open square of the stockade which surrounded the buildings that formed the old fort, a regular prairie fort with corner bastions and a ditch and old brass guns and everything. The scaffold consisted of a platform about twenty feet high with four heavy posts, one at each corner, and two higher posts in the centre with a cross-beam. This had the effect of giving an uninterrupted view from all sides of everything that went on, both on and under the scaffold. Hundreds of Indians from the many reserves surrounding Battleford were gathered to witness the execution, and I am sure very few of the surrounding settlers failed to be present" (in Fryer, 36).

Major Charles A. Boulton: "On the morning of the 27th November, at Battleford, the day broke dark and cloudy, with a frosty air.... The hangings were conducted publicly, and were witnessed by a large number of whites and a few Indians. The Government authorities had permitted Indians from reserves distant ten or fifteen miles from Battleford to be present at the execution, and all night groups of the braves hung about the stores and camped upon the open ground in the vicinity of the barracks of the Mounted Police. Camp-fires lit up the prairies, and the comrades of the warriors to be executed could be heard chanting the death-songs of their tribes.

"Fathers Bigonesse and Cochin remained with the condemned Indians all night" (Bolton, 5).

Constable C. Whitehead: "The whites had all lost friends and relatives in the past unpleasantness, and the different tribes of Indians represented had been practically exterminated, so no very cordial feeling could be looked for. A considerable military force for that time and place was on duty, presumably to prevent trouble. Two full divisions of the NWMP and 'A' battery, in all about 350 men....We were drawn up in the form of a hollow square surrounding the scaffold, and the civilians and Indians were within the stockade, but not allowed to crowd up to the military, but given every opportunity to observe all that happened. Now the scene is set and nothing to do till 10 o'clock" (in Fryer, 36).

William Cameron: "I rose early. Eight o'clock was the hour set for the executions. [Robert] Hodson, the little English cook [for the McLean family at Fort Pitt], ex-prisoner with the McLeans, was executioner.... As I entered the square the death chant of the condemned red men, a weird, melancholy strain, came to me from the guardroom. A group of Cree and Assiniboine Indians sat with their backs against the blacksmith shop in the open space before the scaffold. The authorities, hoping it would have a salutary effect, had allowed a limited number to view the executions. Small knots of civilians conversed in low tones inside the high stockade about the fort; everywhere was that sense of repression always freighting the atmosphere of tragedy. The curtain was about to rise on the final act in the shocking drama which opened eight months before at Frog Lake" (Cameron, 209).

NWMP Fort Battleford Post Journal: "Friday November 27th: Morning opened dull, dark and cloudy, threatening snow.

General parade at 7:30 to form guard during execution of the eight Indians condemned to death.... Mounted men patrolling around Fort. Very cold waiting for prisoners to be bro't from Guard House. At last they appeared about 8:15 AM, with escort of police, prisoner's hands tied behind their backs and wearing black capes with veils to cover their faces. They seemed calm and resigned to their fate, others crazy and excited, most of them assumed a false bravado, don't-care-a-damn sort of air. Miserable Man tried to get up a war song and dance on way to scaffold but it proved a failure."

Alphonse Dion: "Eight hempen ropes hung in readiness for the task at hand on the morning of November 27, 1885…. It was almost eight o'clock in the morning. Grim silence fell over the Indian students of the Battleford Industrial School who were brought in to witness the event. Some of the students were direct relatives of the doomed men on the scaffold, yet they contained their smouldering emotions behind impassive faces" (Dion, 69).

Kamistatum: "What did it matter? The world Wandering Spirit had known was gone forever. War Chiefs were no longer heroes, but bad men. His friends were all gone and his family was hiding in terror. There was no hope left, no more pride, and maybe soon, no more Indians…. The gathered Indians began to sing to their friends and relatives who were to die, a low mournful sound to the hundreds of policemen, soldiers and townspeople also gathered there. The song rose more clearly as each of the doomed men, flanked by policemen, came into sight and were led up the stairs to the gallows platform" (in Goodwill, 77–8).

Constable C. Whitehead: "Comes 10 o'clock. We had been standing in formation since shortly after 9, when we fell in, and we were cold. A weird chanting is heard in the direction of the guard-room, and those of us who could see in that direction find that the prisoners are coming. The chanting gets louder as one by one they emerge from the guard-house, and their voices combine. Their arms are pinioned, but the shackles they have worn since their arrest have been struck off. Each Indian walks between two husky constables — small chance of escape. They look cold — they will be colder soon. They mount the scaffold and are placed by the hangman beneath the dangling rope that awaits each. The hangman places the rope about each neck. The chanting of the 'death song' still goes on" (in Fryer, 36).

William Cameron: "They stepped almost jauntily, dressed in their new suits of brown duck. The weights had been removed from their ankles. Round their shaven scalps were the black caps ready to be drawn over their faces. Immediately in front of them walked Hodson. Intense silence had fallen upon the square, the only sound the measured tramp of the sombre procession" (Cameron, 210).

Major Charles A. Boulton: "The scaffold was so arranged that each man took his place on the trap, side by side. When they were asked if they had anything to say, Wandering Spirit, in his native tongue, acknowledged that he deserved death. He warned his people not to make war on the whites, as they were their friends. He told of the Frog Lake massacre, and took the burden of the crime on himself. He was followed by Miserable Man, who spoke in the same strain" (Boulton, 5).

NWMP Fort Battleford Post Journal: "All ascended the scaffold with comparatively firm step, some silent — while nooses were being adjusted, others singing war songs, Pères Cochin and Bigonesse on scaffold with them to the last."

Father Louis Cochin: "They marched to the place of execution with a firm step, imitating the funeral march of the soldiers who accompanied them. We went to the scaffold with them, where one told me, 'Father … we are anxious to die singing. I pray you to allow us to sing in our style.'… Whilst the ropes were being placed around their necks they sang together. Having observed in the midst of the crowd some relations and friends, they shouted farewell, advising them to forgive their enemies" (in Adams, *Prison of Grass*, 110).

William Cameron: "[W]hile Hodson went round behind them and strapped the ankles of each man together they were told they would be given ten minutes in which to speak, should they feel disposed. All, I think, except Wandering Spirit, availed themselves of the privilege. Little Bear spoke defiantly. He told the Indian onlookers to remember how the whites had treated him — to make no peace with them. The old Assiniboine turned and harangued his companions, urging them to show their contempt for the punishment the government was about to inflict on them. All but Wandering Spirit smiled, sang and shouted short, sharp war-cries" (Cameron, 211).

Joseph Howard: "According to a white witness at the mass execution, the war chief, who had remained mute during his trial, went silent to his death; the Crees, however, say that while the other seven shrieked war songs as the hoods were lowered over their heads, Wandering Spirit hummed a love song to his wife" (Howard, 546).

William Cameron: "The eyes of the Indians looking on grew big: it was easy to see how the words and actions of the doomed men roused in them all the latent savagery bred through generations.... [T]hey neither stirred nor uttered a sound. I glanced over my shoulder from where I stood with notebook and pencil before the scaffold and saw all this" (Cameron, 211).

Constable C. Whitehead: "How is it that sounds and smells live in our memory when taste, feeling and sight are forgotten? I can hear that death chant yet, and the drop of the bodies, when I can easily forget what they looked like....

"The priest who accompanied them is praying, but small attention is accorded him, and the bolt that launches the eight into eternity slips, and the bodies fall" (in Fryer, 36–7).

William Cameron: "The missionaries had sent up their last petitions for the souls of nature's savage and misguided children; a hush fell over all as Hodson stepped behind the still line of dark heads and stooped to draw the bolt. There was a sharp sound of grating iron, the trap dropped, and eight bodies shot through it. A sickening click of dislocated necks, and they hung dangling and gyrating slowly at the ends of as many hempen lines. A few convulsive shudders and all was over ... that awful pause just before the drop is something I am not likely ever to forget" (Cameron, 212).

NWMP Fort Battleford Post Journal: "Nooses fixed, lever pulled and all were in eternity in a second. They died without a struggle and were cut down 10 minutes later, coffined and buried within half an hour. Indian prisoners silent during the day. Moosamin Indian seemed awe inspired. So ended the actors in the Frog Lake massacre...."

Alphonse Dion: "The Indian children of the Industrial School clutched one another. Some let out involuntary sobs for the braves they'd come to admire, now strung out like puppets in a ghastly marionette show. It was all over. The last of the rebel spirits had been smothered. The government had the Indians under control once again" (Dion, 70).

Major Charles A. Boulton: "The Indians who stood at a distance and witnessed the affair were quiet, and immediately after the executions most of them set out for their reserves. Those who remained behind showed no special signs of excitement. Though all must deplore the necessity that arose for setting so severe an example, it was done in the cause of humanity. The lesson that the Indians have been taught has been a severe one and most judicial in its character, but it will do them good in the long run, and render the peace of the country more secure …" (Boulton, 5).

Howard Adams, author: "Every member of the Indian nation heard the death-rattle of the eight heroes who died at the end of the colonizer's rope and they went quietly back to their compounds, obediently submitting themselves to their oppressors. The eight men who sacrificed their lives at the end of the rope were the champions of freedom and democracy. They were incomparable heroes …" (Adams, *Prison*, 109).

Blair Stonechild, interview: "I have heard other people [as well as Howard Adams] argue a similar kind of disappointment, asking why didn't the First Nations also rebel against the oppressor, so to speak? Why didn't they participate fully in the Métis uprising? But this is part of the view that First Nations did actually strongly support Riel, which is something that [Bill Waiser and I] disproved in our book, *Loyal Till Death*.

"Having talked with the elders, I understand that the reason for [not supporting Riel] was because of the treaties. Treaties were compacts or agreements which were tantamount to sacred documents in which a commitment was made to live together in peace. Contrast this with the Métis point of view in which the Métis perceive themselves as a nation which, in the first place, has never been recognized and, therefore, a 'foreign power' has come in and taken over all the resources without recognizing [the nation]: then you can see why you have the kind of outrage that Howard Adams expresses."

Constable C. Whitehead: "Rough pine boxes had been made under the sheriff's orders.... These had been loaded on a wagon for transport to the scene of execution. Unfortunately, the horses bolted and upset the load, and two or three of the boxes were badly broken. In repairing them, the dimensions were increased. The bodies were duly placed in the boxes and we escorted them to the trench that had been excavated in the frozen ground with some difficulty. To our dismay, we found that they would not fit the grave, and we had no tools or dynamite to blast the hole bigger, so it was necessary to put them in sideways. All this took time, and when we had finished, the short day was over" (in Fryer, 38).

Robert Jefferson: "An incident connected with their execution is worth relating. Disposal of the bodies was let by contract but, when it came to the matter of placing the bodies in coffins or boxes, the contractor objected to handling them. This, of course, was to prove his conformity to the prevailing antagonism to 'rebels.' The conflict between duty and inclination was compromised by his placing the boxes below the scaffold, so that when he cut the ropes by which they were suspended the dead Indians dropped into their respective 'caskets.' Then they were hauled to the bank of the river and buried in the sand" (Jefferson, 153).

Douglas Light, author: "They were buried in a large, shallow common grave in a ravine not far from the barracks ... I remember the beautiful fall day, when the Saskatchewan and Battle River hills and valleys were ablaze with colour, that I accompanied William B. Cameron, Sam Swimmer (a nephew of Poundmaker) and William Pritchard to a quiet valley a short distance north of the Mounted Police Barracks at Battleford. We went looking for the burial site that held the remains of the eight Indians who were hung at the fort for their part in the rebellion. When Swimmer and Cameron located the spot, I dug in the loose sand. Imagine my feelings when I located the coffins of the dead in their shallow, common grave. It was a very solemn moment. Swimmer prayed and sang to his departed kinsmen in Cree. As a boy, he had watched these men, his kinsmen, pay the supreme penalty, then be buried in this grave. Cameron stood silently, remembering the events, the faces of the six that he knew, and the trial leading to their execution and burial. We reverently closed the grave and returned to the fort to listen to the stirring tales of this event, one not so very far in the past" (Light, *Footprints in the Dust*, 5–6).

Robert Jefferson: "The Rebellion was over, but it still remained for the losing side to taste the humiliation of the vanquished, and pay the penalty of their rashness. They were helpless and unarmed, so that there was nothing to be feared from them; they were rebels and could be robbed without compunction and with impunity. In this, many in the highest positions set the example and little bands of soldiers and armed civilians scoured the country in search of loot. Whatever of value they found, was appropriated as spoils of war. The detachments of volunteers that remained stationed in Battleford until fall started home so loaded with impedimenta that much had to be abandoned on the road to the railway" (Jefferson, 159).

Walter Hildebrandt:

Big Bear: "The land was not always kind

but gave as it ebbed

We gave back, with thanks in sacrifice

while the whites

only wanted

They took lives without passion.

How could they hang so many men

when they did not know

what I have seen

How could they cut into the river of life"

(in Hildebrandt, *Sightings*, 63).

PROVINCE OF ALBERTA

FROG LAKE MASSACRE
In the isolated area of Frog Lake 35 miles north, nine white people were murdered and two women were taken prisoner on April 2, 1885, at the beginning of the Riel Rebellion. The peaceful morning in Frog Lake village was shattered when the warriors of Big Bear struck down two priests and employees of the Hudson's Bay and the Indian Department. After destroying the village, the Crees fled eastward, but were defeated in battle by the Alberta Field Force. The prisoners were freed and eight of the insurgents hanged.

ELEVEN: THE MEANING OF IT ALL

James G. MacGregor, author: "All was over in a few moments except the burning of the buildings. The Indians took all the supplies and then set fire to the village. All that remained were pieces of charcoal and ashes, and a few tin cans in the old cellars. Today [1949] no traces of a street are visible. The old caved-in cellars, now overgrown with trees, are all that remain to suggest a western town that might have been" (MacGregor, *Blankets & Beads*, 243).

Harold Fryer, author: "Not likely anyone who saw it in 1885 would recognize Frog Lake today [1975]. There is a new hamlet on the reserve, erected during World War Two. It consists of a general store, post office, service station, a few houses. It's a quiet little place where the Indians come to shop and to talk.... Gravel roads now replace the meandering bush trails of yesteryear, broad grain fields the brushland, pick-ups and cars the faithful Indian ponies.

Provincial road sign, Highway 16, Alberta. Photographer: R. Harrington, 1962. (Provincial Archives of Alberta A8637) "Two miles to the east of the hamlet at a fork in the road stands a monument erected in 1925 by the Canadian government in honor of the men slain there. The cairn was unveiled on June 9 of that year by W.B. Cameron" (Fryer, 55).

James G. MacGregor: "In recent years a neat little cemetery has been enclosed by an iron railing, and the Historic Sites Board has erected a cairn to those pioneers who fell at the hands of the Indians they had befriended. From time to time, one may see an old man [W.B. Cameron] taking a party of curious people over the ground" (MacGregor, 243).

William Cameron: "I drew the cord; the flag fluttered down. The cairn, its bronze inscription glowing in the warm sunlight, stood uncovered. The government of the country had paid its tribute to these stalwart pioneers of '85" (Cameron, 225).

MK: The cairn still stands, the bronze and the stone, apparently immutable. A "massacre" occurred here, at the hands of "rebel Indians under Big Bear." A few years ago, visitors were still able to read explanatory placards, since removed, which offered much newer interpretations of the event; these were not attributed. "*Who can sell the land?*" read one such placard. "*Who can buy it? By 1885 the native people of the west were in hard times.*" The text was barely legible and in parts erased. "*Big Bear did not want war. That was brought on by his war chief, Wandering Spirit, a striking, charismatic man.... Some of the rebels escaped south of the 'medicine line.' Those who surrendered or were captured were tried in white man's court and given the white man's justice. Big Bear went to prison for the sins of his followers.*" A few years ago, a faded purple cloth, a cloth offering, hung on the branch of a poplar tree just inside the cemetery fence. And so this little scene was a visible representation of all the ways in which we talk about "Frog Lake" in our own time. On the one hand, the official, long-standing version of tragedy visited upon stalwart (white) pioneers by "rebel" Indians. On the other hand, the unofficial, First Nations' perspective on land, suffering, grievance, violence, and retribution. Gradually, the one has yielded to the other, or, rather, the two have come to overlap or intersect in complex relationships of perspective, memory, rights, and politics.

WITNESSES OF 1885

Theresa Delaney: "There is one thing I do know and most emphatically desire to express and have thoroughly understood, and that is the fact, *the Indians have no grievances and no complaints to make.* Their treatment is of the best and most generous kind. The government spares no pains to attempt to make them adopt an agricultural life, to teach them to rely upon their own strength, to become independent people and good citizens.... They need never want for food. Their rations are most regularly dealt out to them and they are paid to clear and cultivate their own land.... The Indians have nothing to complain of and as a race they are happy in their quiet home of the wilderness and I consider it a great shame for evil-minded people, whether whites or half-breeds, to instil into their excitable heads the false idea that they are persecuted by the government" (Delaney, 62).

MK: Delaney wrote this in retrospect, safely back in the bosom of her Ontario family, and, who knows, mindful of the expectations public opinion held regarding what, if anything, Indians had to "complain of." Yet it was commonly believed, as Charles Mulvany, writing in 1885, believed, that they had risen up in rebellion, and shown their true nature. "The demon of anarchy and rebellion becomes tenfold more horrible when he possesses the breasts of those rude tribes who have never learned to respect the usages of civilized warfare.... On the 2nd of April the massacre took place under circumstances which will always stamp it as one of the most cruel and treacherous in the annals of Indian warfare" (Mulvany, 89). There were even some First Nations commentators among Big Bear's own people at the time who seemed to concur, if only despairingly, with this assessment of their cruelty; so the *Toronto Mail* reported on July 2, 1885: "We are doomed, and will be killed one after another by the whites. But before we die, or disappear altogether, we must enjoy ourselves as much as we possibly can, and therefore we must plunder stores and kill as many white people as we can" (in Dempsey, 160).

Sarah Carter, interview: "In whose interests was it that this be the official version of events? My answer to that would be that it was the result of a variety of institutions and pressures: governments, politicians, and the military. It was certainly in the interests of the Canadian government and their business supporters. *Two Months in the Camp of Big Bear* came out in November 1885, and it was in that very month that the hanging of Riel took place [November 16] and then a very short week later [November 27] the eight Aboriginal men at the Battleford barracks.

"And *Two Months* was not only published in November, it was also serialized in at least one newspaper in Ontario. I believe it had a significant role to play in justifying these very harsh measures in keeping the so-called savagery before the public — an outburst of 'inexplicable' savagery that the government took absolutely no responsibility for. Instead, it kept in people's minds the idea of a peaceful community of innocent settlers, and the inexplicable, sudden outburst of savagery."

MK: But even among the victims of the violence — for example the other

Theresa taken hostage, Theresa Gowlanlock, also writing in retrospect from the parental home — another perspective was already available if only tentatively: "Who was to blame? who was the cause? direct or indirect, it is not my intention or desire to say: suffice it is to note, that there was discontent; and therefore there must have been grievances, and an attempt should have been made or an understanding arrived at, whereby this state of discontent should have been replaced by that of content, without disturbance. Where there is discontent there must be badness and suffering, with evils and excesses lying in its wake. To have removed those grievances was the imperative duty of the dispensers of the law and order ... but it was not done in time and the inevitable did come swift and sure; the innocent were made to feel its fury" (Gowanlock, 38).

Almost a century later, as if to take up Gowanlock's point and against his great-aunt's, Theresa Delaney, writer Robert Fulford signalled the direction that Canadian public opinion was veering when it stopped to think about the historical relations of First Nations and white settlers.

Robert Fulford, author: "Aunt Theresa doesn't bother to deny any land claims the Indians may have had; she doesn't mention them. She assumes that the Indians must and will become farmers, assimilated to white society under the kindly direction of good men like her late husband. She notes with regret that those she knew during her three years in the North-West had the unfortunate habit of taking a month off every spring and fall to hunt, each time counting the weeks till their freedom came. In her view the government was if anything too kind to them, and 'the Indians have no grievances and no complaints to make.' She wrote those words, carefully italicizing them for emphasis, just a few months after her husband died in her arms from a bullet fired by an Indian. Like a Bourbon, she learned nothing and forgot nothing.

"Aunt Theresa moved back to the Ottawa Valley. She never married again.... My father, who knew her slightly, never mentioned that she was bitter or broken. He spoke of her with affection, as the family's celebrity. Reading her words, as I've done occasionally over the last twenty-five years, I've often wished she had been more curious, more questioning, more fore-sighted — an exception to something evil rather than an example of it. Still, I've always been grateful to have her. Nobody else in our family ever did anything nearly so exciting" (Fulford, 1).

THE REVISED HISTORY

MK: In 1936, introducing his now-classic *The Birth of Western Canada: A History of the Riel Rebellions*, George F.G. Stanley made the case for a new interpretation of the dramatic events of 1885. Breaking with the political, racial, and religious "prejudices of Old Canada," he suggested that the rebellions were a manifestation in western Canada of a universal phenomenon: "Namely, the clash between primitive and civilized peoples. In all parts of the world, in South Africa, New Zealand and North America, the penetration of white settlement into territories inhabited by Native peoples has led to friction and wars; Canadian expansion into the North-West led to a similar result" (Stanley, *vii*). Eventually the vocabulary of this argument would be refined but the crucial point had been made: in the encounter of First Nations peoples with the relentlessly expansionist Europeans, their resistance was foreordained.

George F.G. Stanley: "To add to the Indian resentment against the whites, a realization of their fundamental error as to the real meaning of the treaties began to penetrate the Indian mind. In few cases had they understood the full import of the treaties to which they had so readily affixed their totems. To them, as to many savage tribes, the western notion of private property in land was entirely foreign. Among the Indians the idea prevailed that the white men had come to 'borrow' their land, not to buy it" (Stanley, 275).

MK: A generation later, in 1983, the historian Thomas Flanagan underscored the political import of the Métis rebellion on the prairies under the leadership of Louis Riel: "He [Riel] held that the Metis were the true owners of the North-West" (Flanagan, 86). And, taking up from Stanley and Flanagan, with a post-colonial twist in a history course offered in 2004 at the University of Calgary, historian Sarah Carter agreed that "the events of 1885 are part of a broader pattern of resistance to colonial rule. In the late nineteenth century in many parts of the globe, the land of Indigenous people was claimed/seized by European powers, and in many locations Indigenous people strove to protect their autonomy through resistance and rebellion." The scholarly technique is *comparative history* and its concept is *transnational history*. This perspective of anti-colonialist resistance was not unique to white historians and writers. In 1951, in an article prepared "many years ago," Edward Ahenakew wrote of his thoughts at the site of the Frog Lake Massacre.

"Because I know the Crees, I do not put it [the massacre] down to sheer blood-thirstiness.... Imagine a people who have lived and roamed over this great North Western land, breathing in the freedom of the prairies at every breath, their will never questioned and kept in bounds only by the teaching of the old men of the nation, knowing most exactingly the ways of the country, skilful in everything which pertained to the making of their livelihood, conquering the necessarily hard conditions under which they lived, feeling the manhood that was in their bodies. Such people must love freedom as did their God-given animal, the noble buffalo. They must resent anything that tends to bring that freedom to nought, or even to restrict it. It is only nature, it were unnatural if it were not so....

"To me, the massacre at Frog Lake and the participation in the Rebellion, came in the natural course of events. The eight mounds at Frog Lake are evidence of the last attempt of the Indian to register his disapproval of the ever-increasing power of another race in the land" (in Hughes, 353-4, 356).

BIRTH OF THE FREEDOM FIGHTER AT FROG LAKE

MK: In the voice of the Cree elder, Old Keyam, the embattled Cree of Big Bear's band, whose freedom "was intense and vital to them," have become the "last resisters of the white man's power." He acknowledges that "the story is becoming almost legendary, yet it is not so far removed in the past as to have made it impossible for me to have heard accounts from men who were eye-witnesses" (Ahenakew, 71-2). One of the most dramatic revisions to have been made to the official record arose precisely from these witnesses — some re-assembled here, in this *Reader* — in their evaluation of the character and actions of the Plains Cree chief Big Bear. Far from being the hideous war chief intent on the murder of innocent white people, Big Bear was known to his own people, and to those whites who were close to him, as a man of peace. He was described in the

Saskatchewan Herald as early as 1879 as "the head and soul of all our Canadian Plains Indians" (in Stonechild & Waiser, 106) and in war council as a negotiator, even with hostages on his hands.

Fred Horse: "All those white men and white women, no one is to kill them, any of them, was the ruling made, and agreed on by all. We will keep them alive. When everything settles, and nothing more happens, we will set them free. Oh! They made a good rule. No one is to get killed" (in Stonechild, 28).

MK: Yet, it was also known that Big Bear was losing authority among his people to the young warriors. Referring to the newspaper and court reports of the time, historian Hugh Dempsey summarized the situation just before the violence was unleashed in Frog Lake.

Hugh Dempsey: "Big Bear had already lost his fight to stay out of treaty; lost his fight to avoid taking a reserve; lost the leadership of his band; now, he had lost his chance for the Crees to negotiate for a better treaty and a better deal from the Canadian government — all because of Wandering Spirit's hatred of the white man, of Imasees' desire to be chief, of alcohol in the form of painkiller and sacramental wine, of the disappearance of the buffalo and starvation, of anger and frustration at being ground under the heel of an unfeeling government" (Dempsey, 159–60).

MK: In the mayhem that ensued, "Big Bear's last dreams were shattered, destroyed forever in the hail of bullets that had left nine bodies scattered amid the chaos of what had been a peaceful village" (Dempsey, 159).

Peaceful village? That perspective has in turn been revised. According to Dempsey's own account — of why Frog Lake, and not other settlements, had come under such violent attack — Big Bear's followers who camped out near Frog Lake were hungry, depressed, and angry in part because of the treatment meted out by some of the Frog Lake settlers, notably the Indian agent and farm instructor, and because of grudges, jealousies, quarrels, and the desire for vengeance.

In an appendix to his history of the Métis Nation in the Northwest, Auguste-Henri de Trémaudan quotes from a "special report" by Lawrence Clarke, HBC chief factor at Fort Carlton in 1885 (no source given): "Men of brutish instincts were appointed farm instructors to the Indians. Their maltreatment of these poor people was brutal; they responded to them with kicks and punches, accompanied by the most disgusting curses.... Let a Commission or Committee of Parliament be called and I'll be prepared to describe to the people of Canada such a state of affairs that they'll be amazed a revolt hadn't broken out years ago" (Trémaudan, 185; MK trans.).

Howard Adams: "It is easy to understand how hostility could have developed among the Indians who were being continuously humiliated and brutalized by their oppressors in return for barely enough rations for survival. There was no redress for these grievances. The Indians were probably watching for their opportunity to make a thrust for freedom, and the Duck Lake victory on March 26 sparked this thrust. It seems obvious that the Indians chose their victims according to their oppressiveness.

"[citing Trémaudan] 'Quinn drank rather freely, and when he was drunk he liked to stage a "power play." In the middle of winter, he denied rations to the Indians unless they cut cordwood.... The real reason for this inhuman act was that Tom Quinn and Delaney, the agricultural instructor, wanted to clear the land that they coveted as future "homesteads" after the Indians had left for the reserves.'

"[The Indians'] war was against those white men who held them in subjugation, and not against white people in general. They knew precisely who were their colonizers. It was not an accident that they disposed of Quinn, the Indian agent, and Delaney, the farm instructor, and the two priests. This was not an act of revenge; it was a struggle against colonization, a historical development" (Adams, *Prison*, 108).

MK: As for the punishment dealt the warriors of Big Bear's band, Adams continues, "public scaffolds in the streets of Regina and North Battleford" [actually on the parade ground within Fort Battleford] "that snapped the necks of Indian and Métis heroes had to be the most extraordinary instruments of violence and terror. Why should colonized victims be expected to submit willingly to brutality and torture? In an effort to liberate his people in 1885, Wandering Spirit, an Indian of Frog Lake Reserve" [actually a war chief of Big Bear's Band] "killed a priest and Indian agent, the two white oppressors terrorizing his community. This was an act of heroism on behalf of his people" (Adams, *Tortured People*, 2).

In his book published in 1999, Adams had if anything condensed this view to a succinct condemnation of "the vilest of Euro-Canadian imperialism," with its "predatory thrust" of war and terror on the peoples of the territories invaded and captured by "the Ottawa Regime with its mercenaries and machine guns" (Adams, *Tortured People*, 2).

MK: The "predatory thrust" concluded in the final sequestration of the Indians onto the reserves, in the amendments to the Indian Act that criminalized dances and ceremonies, in the removal of mixed-race persons from the treaties who, under the pressure of their poverty, handed in their scrip (certificate of entitlement to land) for cash and supplies, and, finally, in the offer of "free" homestead land to European and Canadian settlers.

Old Keyam: "And settlers, who had come at first only in small groups, came by the hundreds and thousands when the railroad was built. These people regarded the Indians, sometimes with fear, sometimes with derision. Only a few came to know us, or could possibly do so, for we were living then on reserves.... We were hobbled like horses, limited to our reserves, and quite unfitted for any life outside..... Government agents were no wiser in their turn, for many of them were small men who owed their position to political patronage alone, who used the law to become despots in their own areas ..." (in Ahenakew, 72).

Sarah Carter, interview: "Even before 1885 with the problems of weather, frost, and fire, prairie fire, there was a lot of difficulty in enticing people to move west. A lot was invested in this whole project in the west — the huge Dominion Land Survey, the construction of the railway, and *Two Months in the Camp of Big Bear* was used to demonstrate that there had to be new and determined efforts to keep Aboriginal people and newcomers apart, and to segregate them. And I believe it was in the interests of elites to demonstrate that this was necessary and that if this could be done, newcomers would be attracted to the west.

"And, after 1885, the numbers of surveillance agents on reserves increases dramatically — the number of farm instructors and Indian agents and agencies increased. There's a new pass system that's put into place. It was put in place in a modest way in 1885 but it does become a regular feature, especially on the prairie reserves in the areas of intensive settlement — a pass system that prevents people from moving off their reserves.

"Also, the North West Mounted Police, their numbers are increased dramatically after 1885. So, there is a lot more emphasis on monitoring First Nations people both on and off their reserves.

"1885 was a very important watershed in western Canada in very many ways. Both Métis and First Nations people before 1885 had been insisting that they were Aboriginal people and they had a right to share in the future prosperity of this land. This didn't sit well with a lot of people, both before 1885 and after. But after[wards] they seized on all these events and elaborated and embroidered them and insisted on the official version to insist that both Métis and First Nations people could not be seen as people who should share in the future prosperity of the land. They were seen as menacing savages, backward, and as a people who had to be contained and restrained on reserves, and, in the case of the Métis, their influence had to be undermined and broken up."

LAYING BLAME

MK: In the eyes of many Canadians, the First Nations peoples of the plains had been demonized by their association with the events of war: looting and pillage, murder and hostage-taking, and the treasonous use of arms against the lawful authorities of state and army. But, in an argument that would be taken up and fully developed a century later, the white teacher and settler who lived among the Indians of Battleford, Robert Jefferson, wondered how a charge of treason could be fastened on an Indian. "They are not subjects of the Crown, but allies, and a treaty was made with them as such. True, they broke that treaty, but treaties are abrogated every once in a while by civilized nations, without the determination being treated as rebellion. There must be some way out of this difficulty, but that way will always remain to me one of the mysteries of the law" (Jefferson, 156).

The "mystery" had much to do with the confusion, in many minds and in the popular press, of the Métis insurgents under Louis Riel and their military campaigns in the Northwest against the Canadian army, with the events at Frog Lake, Fort Pitt, and Frenchman Butte, which involved not the Métis but the Plains and Wood Cree. All were lumped together as perpetrators of violence and treachery. As recently as 1985, on the hundredth anniversary of the Frog Lake Massacre, residents in and around Frog Lake were anxious to set the record straight with reporter Rita Feutl:

> Francis Dufresne, who lives next door to Frog Lake on the Fishing Lake Métis Settlement (population is just under 500) insisted the Métis played no role in the massacre. 'It was the Indians who did it.' Yes it was, agrees Margaret Quinney, in her home on the Frog Lake Indian Reserve which counts less than 1000 people as its members; but it wasn't the Indians *from* the reserve who committed the murders. 'They ought to call it the Big Bear Tribe's Massacre,' she said emphatically (Feutl, 54).

And indeed it was warriors of Big Bear's band who were among those who were hanged for the deaths at Frog Lake. But, even when controversial, recent scholarship of historians such as Blair Stonechild and Bill Waiser opens up the historical record to reveal a more complex situation. Lorraine Freeman, writing at the Métis Resource Centre, reminds us that "it is important we remember that it was First Nations as well as the Métis fighting to protect the rights of Aboriginal peoples of the North West." But Stonechild and Waiser, co-authors of *Loyal Till Death: Indians and the North-West Rebellion*, argue that the First Nations played a unique role in the events of 1885, and they cite the late John Tootoosis, president of the Federation of Saskatchewan Indians, who said, in 1984: "When the Métis people were preparing to have this uprising, they [the Indian people] all said no. We can't support you. We signed an agreement with the Crown not to fight any more; they were to live in peace with these people. We signed a treaty, we have to live up to this treaty" (in Stonechild & Waiser, 3).

In fact, most of the Treaty Indians of the Northwest took this commitment so seriously that they remained neutral throughout the troubles. Pacifism, not war, was the main "narrative," even among many Métis.

Heather Devine, interview: "Traditionally, those individuals in Native communities who do not perceive themselves to be wronged may or may not have felt obliged to participate in revenge raids or killings or in defence of other individuals unless they were relatives. The practice was 'do not hinder but do not help.' That is, maintain your neutrality. If your cousin wants to settle a score with somebody, that's fine, that's his business. But that doesn't mean you have to assist."

Joseph Dion: "The final surrender was brought about, not because the Indians of the West had been defeated into submission, nor that the fight had been knocked out of them. The fact of the matter was that the great majority of the natives, Metis included, remained neutral, and many were inclined to favour the whites. Most of the Chipewyans, for instance, next door neighbours of the Crees at Frog Lake, remained hidden throughout the conflict.... Among the many Crees at Saddle Lake, only a very few of the more adventurous members took part at all in the rebellion.... The large settlement of Metis and Crees at Lac La Biche never moved....

"The history of the West would be vastly different today [1950s] had all our elders and headmen lost control, as in the case of poor old Big Bear. His men murdered helpless people, and especially the two priests, thus rendering him an outcast whose band had to fight alone" (Dion, 102–3).

MK: But what of the accused, the imprisoned, and the hanged? How are they to be regarded now?

Blair Stonechild, interview: "While it's clear that Riel committed specific actions that were against law, as Wandering Spirit and the other individuals did, there is a larger context. This isn't simply 'breaking laws.' These are people who are responding to a larger sense of injustice, one which exists at the level of the state: in the one case, the failure to recognize the Métis nation and rights, and, in the other case, the broken treaties and the failure to give First Nations administrative justice on the same level as other individuals."

MK: In August 1973, at the unveiling of a historical plaque at Fort Pitt, Big

Bear's grandson, Four Souls, of Rocky Boy, Montana, delivered
a blistering defense of the accused of Frog Lake:

Four Souls: "If we are going to exonerate Riel, what about Wandering
Spirit and the men hanged alongside him? And if we can't
bring ourselves to absolve them, what about the approximately fifty other Indians convicted of treason — felony for
their actions during the rebellion? Most of them served terms
of three to seven years at Stony Mountain Penitentiary north
of Winnipeg. Prison ruined the health of many of them. Some
died there, others were released near death. Yet, most were
wrongfully convicted, which is evident from reading trial
transcripts preserved in Canada Sessional Papers of 1885 and
1886.... 'Since the conviction of Big Bear,' said exasperated
defence lawyer Beverly Robertson, 'I have felt it almost a hopeless task to obtain from a jury in Regina a fair consideration
of the case of an Indian. It has seemed to me only necessary
to say in this town to a jury, there is an Indian, and we will
put him in the dock to convict him.' If our politicians want to
right old wrongs, they should begin by pardoning these men,
not Louis Riel'" (www.sicc.ca/saskindian).

WHAT IS TO BE DONE?

MK: While the question of whether or not to have Louis Riel officially
pardoned or exonerated for treason — the charge for which he
was hanged in 1885 — has been aired repeatedly, especially
since the centenary of his execution, there has been relatively
muted public discussion about the fate of the Aboriginal men
also executed in 1885.

Blair Stonechild, interview: "How many Canadians are aware of the fact that the hangings actually happened? How many Canadians are aware that this is the largest mass hanging in Canadian history? Because it's not really talked about, it's not explained. I think it's definitely something which is unresolved. Part of the key to unlocking this is to look again at the role of Big Bear, and whether he should now be pardoned. People are talking about the pardon of Riel, why aren't they talking about Big Bear? I think his case is just as good, if not better."

MK: Part of the difficulty in having the discussion is the language in which it has been conventionally treated. For instance, the historic site has been known officially as the Frog Lake Massacre Site, but the Alberta provincial government has announced plans to change this to the Frog Lake Historic Site, deleting the contentious word *massacre*. But if it wasn't a massacre (defined by the Canadian Oxford as "general slaughter"), what *did* occur at Frog Lake? Murder? Killings? War crimes? Uprising?

Blair Stonechild, interview: "The word *murder*, of course, has all kinds of connotations, and fits quite well with the prejudices of the day — the prevailing attitude of the time that First Nations were simply savages and with no real system of moral values or intellectual thinking. Therefore, it was quite expected of them that, faced by the situation they were in, they would simply jump up and kill people. That fit in quite well with the prevailing stereotype. It's part of the challenge to try and get a new view of the events. But you don't do that overnight."

Heather Devine, interview: "As historians, we're always concerned with terminology and the use of terms which might be perceived as inflammatory. The term *massacre* is inflammatory when it is used in conjunction with Aboriginal people. It evokes certain

THE FROG LAKE READER - *Myrna Kostash*

images that are stereotypic and negative and also in some cases may be inaccurate in terms of what took place during the event. When I talk about Frog Lake I prefer to use the term *killings* rather than *massacre* because I do not believe that it was premeditated. And I don't think it was a *battle*; it was not a battle.

"But nor would I describe this event as being *murder*. When I think of murder, I think of a premeditated situation where there is a motive. In this particular situation, there may have been some general discontent and resentment that was long-simmering, and drug and alcohol impairment, and if I were to pick a word to describe it, I would use the legal term, *manslaughter*, for situations where someone dies as a result of violence 'without malice aforethought.' That, I think, would be a more precise and appropriate way to describe it. But you can't go calling it 'the Frog Lake Manslaughter'!"

MK: Rudy Wiebe has been described as a "mythologizer" of Big Bear and readily admits to having been deeply affected by his reading of William Cameron's *Blood Red the Sun* and the image of the frantic chief, Big Bear, rushing towards his tribesmen as the killing begins at Frog Lake and yelling at the top of his voice, "*Tesqua! Tesqua!* (Stop! Stop!)." But Wiebe is also able to enter the minds and hearts of the young warriors.

Rudy Wiebe, interview: "In one sense, Frog Lake is a simple event of a proud people pushed down into poverty and into starvation. As a warrior, you're not thinking ahead very far, but at the same time you are responsible for feeding your people. So, you can understand what drove them. But at the same time you cannot justify in any sense their killing ten defenceless people, including two priests in the process of holding their religious ceremonies. That is unjustifiable. Big Bear never justified it, to anyone; he was as saddened as anyone by those events. So perhaps by just sweeping it under the carpet we have not really resolved or talked about this. Every once in a while a historian talks about it briefly but there is no wider discussion about it like there is about what happened at Batoche.

"As Canada's relations with Japanese-Canadians, and now with Ukrainian-Canadians, prove, these tragedies, these horrors, sit there in our lives, and maybe at some point we should just talk about them openly, bring them to public witness. And then we can deal with them. They were long ago and we can't change the facts, but we can talk them through. This is what human beings do, they talk things through until they come to some kind of understanding among themselves. And that's the way we resolve problems, we don't go around shooting people. You cannot change history but what we can do about history is talk about it and try to understand it.

"We haven't talked about it enough, I don't think."

Heather Devine, interview: "I have the frustration that a lot of historians have, in that so often people want nice easy answers to complex questions. They want to be able to understand events in the past in a simple way. But, in fact, these events were very complex. They were many-faceted events. We weren't there. We rely on a wide variety of sources that we have to evaluate in terms of their validity. Then we have to try to take all of these sources, whether they be oral historical accounts, trial transcripts, homesteaders' accounts — we have to take all this material and from it try to distill a narrative that somehow reflects some sort of truth about what happened.

"But people have to understand that this process [of determining an accurate sequence of events] is highly complex; the people of 1885 would have had difficulty in reaching any kind of consensus about what was happening — and they were *there*. They were too close to it. And we're still, in many ways, too close to it now.

"It wasn't that long ago."

Mass grave of First Nations warriors near
Battleford, SK. Photo taken by the author.

CHRONOLOGY OF EVENTS

1876	Left out of the original negotiations, Big Bear refuses to sign Treaty Six.
1882	John Delaney, farm instructor, and wife, Theresa, arrive in Frog Lake; Big Bear accepts Treaty Six but not a reserve.
WINTER, 1884–85	Big Bear's band camps at Frog Lake near a Wood Cree reserve; Theresa Gowanlock arrives in Frog Lake, joining husband, John, grist mill owner-operator.

1885

MARCH 19	Métis elect provisional government at Batoche under leadership of Louis Riel.
MARCH 26	**Battle of Duck Lake.**
MARCH 31	Council of Provisional Government moves Métis force to Batoche.
APRIL 2	(Holy Thursday) Killings at Frog Lake.
APRIL 3	(Good Friday) Frog Lake hostages absorbed into Big Bear's camp; Mann family arrives in Fort Pitt.
APRIL 4	Trader Henry Ross Halpin brought in as hostage from Cold Lake.
APRIL 13	Inspector Francis Dickens sends out David Cowan, Clarence Loasby, and Henry Quinn to scout for Big Bear.
APRIL 14/15	Cree siege of Fort Pitt; Cowan shot; NWMP escape.
APRIL 17	Hostages from Fort Pitt, including family of W.J. McLean, moved to Frog Lake.

APRIL 19 Hostages reach the camp.

APRIL 20 Major General T.B. Strange leaves Calgary for Edmonton.

APRIL 26 Father Legoff and Chipewyan band arrive in Big Bear's camp.

MAY 1 Strange arrives in Edmonton.

MAY 15 Cree leave Frog Lake proceeding for Frenchman Butte to join Poundmaker; Riel surrenders.

MAY 24 Strange sets up base at Fort Pitt.

MAY 26 Poundmaker surrenders at Fort Battleford.

MAY 27 Strange and his men of the Alberta Field Force leave Fort Pitt for Frenchman Butte.

MAY 28 **Battle of Frenchman Butte**; hostages moved away for safety; Father Legoff and people flee for Catholic mission in Cold Lake.

JUNE 1 Theresa Gowanlock, Theresa Delaney, John Pritchard, and André Nault escape; William Cameron escapes separately.

JUNE 2 McLeans and Cree bands reach Loon (Makwa) Lake, Sam Steele in pursuit.

JUNE 3 **Battle of Loon Lake**; Gowanlock and Delaney found by scouts out of Battleford.

JUNE 4 Steele meets up with General Frederick Middleton's column, pursues Cree who flee Loon Lake.

JUNE 7 Wood Cree with McLeans separate from Plains Cree band and strike north to Beaver River.

JUNE 9 Middleton orders withdrawal from Loon (Makwa) Lake back to Fort Pitt.

JUNE 18 McLeans released.

JUNE 22 Released hostages arrive at Fort Pitt.

JULY 2 Big Bear, accompanied by his son, Horse Child, and a councillor, All and a Half, surrenders at Fort Carlton.

JULY 20 Wandering Spirit surrenders at Fort Pitt.

NOVEMBER 16 Louis Riel hanged in Regina.

NOVEMBER 22 Trial of Cree and Assiniboine men at Fort Battleford.

NOVEMBER 27 Mass hanging of eight condemned at Fort Battleford.

BIOGRAPHIES OF CITED WRITERS

Graeme Mercer Adam (1830–1912): Scottish-born publisher in Toronto and prolific writer of popular Canadian history.

Howard Adams (1926–2001): Saskatchewan Métis scholar and activist; his great-grandfather Maxime Lepine and great-uncle Ambroise Lepine stood with Métis leader Louis Riel during the Northwest Rebellion. Author of *Prison of Grass* and *A Tortured People*.

Reverend Edward Ahenakew (1885–1961): Anglican clergyman born on the Sandy Lake Indian Reserve, educated in Saskatchewan mission schools, and at theological colleges in Toronto and Saskatoon. Speaker and writer in Cree and English, author of *Voices of the Plains Cree*.

Bob Beal (1949–): Former newspaper reporter and editor, now a historian and writer who specializes in the history of western Canada and in Indian treaties, and who works in First Nations litigation. Author with Rod Macleod of *Prairie Fire: The 1885 North-West Rebellion*.

Alexander Begg (1839–1897): Born in Quebec City, moved west for business reasons to the Red River settlement (Manitoba) in 1867. Vigorous advocate for representative government for the people and was at first was supportive of both the Métis and Hudson's Bay Company; later, editor of the *Victoria Daily News*.

Charles Arkoll Boulton (1841–1899): In 1869 he was assigned to a survey party sent to the Red River Settlement; involved in an attempt to put down an uprising by Louis Riel. In 1885, led a group of militia known as Boulton's Scouts to help put down the Northwest Rebellion.

David Breen (1960–): BC-based historian of ranching and petroleum industries of Alberta.

Brian Brennan (1943–): Calgary-based author of popular social history of western Canada, including *The Good Steward: The Story of Ernest C. Manning* and *Scoundrels and Scallywags: Characters from Alberta's Past.*

Wayne Brown (1941–): Retired Alberta Fish and Wildlife officer, author of *Steele's Scouts: Samuel Benfield Steele and the North-West Rebellion.* Member of the Frenchman Butte Museum committee, which seeks renovation of the historic site.

William Bleasdell Cameron (1862–1951): Arrived in Battleford from Ontario in 1881 at nineteen; first job carrying supplies was on a Red River cart brigade; in Frog Lake, as clerk with the HBC trader. Later, a professional writer and editor of *Field and Stream* in New York City.

Sarah Carter (1954–): Historian of western Canada at the University of

Alberta, the author of several books that examine the history of settlement, gender relations, and Aboriginal-European interaction in western Canada, including *Capturing Women: The Manipulation of Cultural Imagery in Canada's Prairie West* and *Lost Harvests: Prairie Indian Reserve Farmers and Government Policy*.

Guillaume Charette (1884–1952): Manitoba Métis, graduated from the Faculty of Law at the University of Manitoba, Charette was employed as a federal civil servant and was active as the president of L'Union Nationale Métisse.

Jimmy Chief: Son of one of Little Bear's (Apischakskoos) daughters; hanged for the murder of George Dill at Frog Lake. Chief was interviewed by Edgar Mapletoft in *Fort Pitt Unfolding*.

Father Louis Cochin (1856–1927): Oblate missionary among the Cree, based on Poundmaker's reserve.

Mel Dagg (1941–): BC-based author of *Four Wheel Drift: New and Selected Stories* and *The Women on the Bridge*.

Charles Daoust (1865–1924): In 1885, a member of Regiment Carabiniers, Mont-Royal 65th.

Theresa Delaney (1865?–1913): Married John Delaney in 1882; settled in Frog Lake, worked as a "farm instructress" to the Wood Cree women, giving lessons in baking, milking, knitting, and dressmaking. Returned to Ontario in 1885.

Hugh Dempsey (1929–): Chief curator emeritus of the Glenbow Museum in Calgary, a journalist and popular historian who combines oral history with documentary sources.

Heather Devine (1955–): Historian specializing in Canadian native history, American Indian policy, and western-Canadian ethnic history at the University of Calgary; author of *The People Who Own Themselves: Aboriginal Ethnogenesis in a Canadian Family, 1660–1900*.

Francis Jeffrey Dickens (1844–1886): Aka 'Chickenstalker,' son of Charles Dickens the novelist; 1874, appointed Inspector in the NWMP, saw service at Swan River, at posts along the Saskatchewan and south to Forts Walsh and Macleod and finally back to the Saskatchewan at Forts Battleford and Pitt.

Alphonse Dion: No information.

Joseph Dion (1888–1960): Cree schoolteacher, born into a family that witnessed the events at Frog Lake and Frenchman Butte, 1885; organizer of the Indian Association of Alberta and of the Métis Association, active in preserving their history. His grandmother was Mary Dion.

John George Donkin (1853–1890): Left Liverpool for Canada in 1884; volunteered with NWMP in 1885. Later returned to England to work as a journalist.

David R. Elliott (19??–): Historian of western-Canadian social and intellectual trends, and co-author of *Bible Bill: A Biography of William Aberhart*.

Lee Elliott (1954–): Lives in Edmonton and has published poems and short stories in *Fiddlehead* and *Other Voices*.

Peter Erasmus (1833–1931): Fluent in six Aboriginal languages, Peter Erasmus was the Métis interpreter at the Treaty Six negotiations, a guide and assistant to the Palliser expedition, and to Methodist missionaries, and a trader, hunter, Indian agent, farmer, and mission worker.

Rita Feutl (1959–): Edmonton journalist and author of *Rescue at Fort Edmonton*, historical fiction for young adults.

Lorraine Freeman (19??–): Founder, past president, and executive director of the Métis Resource Culture and Heritage Resource Centre Inc. in Winnipeg.

Harold Fryer (1923–?): Peace River area writer.

Robert Fulford (1932–): Canadian writer, editor, journalist, critic, and columnist.

Bill Gallaher (19??–): Victoria-based singer and songwriter, and author of *The Frog Lake Massacre* and *The Journey: The Overlanders' Quest for Gold.*

Jean Goodwill (1928–1997): Born Jean Cuthand on the Little Pine Reserve; graduated as an RN in Prince Albert, Saskatchewan; a founding member of the Native Women's Association of Canada. As the daughter of John Tootoosis, who was born in 1899 on Poundmaker Reserve, Saskatchewan, she transcribed his story from Cree.

Theresa Gowanlock (1863–1899): Born in Lincoln County in the Niagara Peninsula into a pioneering farming family. In 1884 moved to Frog Lake with husband John. Returned to Ontario in 1885.

William Antrobus Griesbach (1878–1945): **Army officer, city alderman, and then mayor in Edmonton and federal senator; author of** *I Remember,* **a reminiscence.**

Henry Ross Halpin (1856–1930): **Served in the HBC post at Cold Lake, a branch post of Fort Pitt; during the siege of Fort Pitt, served as Big Bear's secretary. Then joined the Alberta Field Force as a scout, helping track the Cree. At the trial of Big Bear, spoke in his favour, saying the chief was innocent of the murders at Frog Lake.**

Robert W. Hendriks (1939–): **Historian and retired teacher, Alberta-based, author of biography of William B. Cameron,** *A Life of Writing and Adventure.*

Walter Hildebrandt (1951–): **Historian, poet, and director of Athabasca University Press; author of** *Views from Battleford: Constructed Visions of an Anglo-Canadian West* **and** *The Cypress Hills: The Land and Its People.*

Fred Horse: **Cree elder, informant to Jean Goodwill and Blair Stonechild; grandson of Kamistatum.**

John Horse (1873–1959): **Father of Fred Horse, gave an account of the Frog Lake Massacre in 1926. An almost identical version by Fred Horse was published by the Saskatchewan Indian Federated College in 1985.**

Joseph Kinsey Howard (1906–1951): **American (Montana) author of the landmark biography** *Strange Empire: Louis Riel and the Metis People.*

Robert Jefferson (1857–1934): **British immigrant to Canada, moved in 1878 west to Battleford, then the capital of the NWT; married sister of Poundmaker and worked as a teacher on the Red Pheasant reserve for six years.**

D'arcy Jenish (1952–): **Ontario-based biographer of the explorer David Thompson, and author of *Indian Fall: The Last Great Days of the Plains Cree and the Blackfoot Confederacy.***

Vernon LaChance: **Editor of Francis Dicken's Fort Pitt diary.**

Patrick Gammie Laurie (1833–1903): **Newspaperman in Battleford when it was recently named capital of the North-West Territories; walked 1430 KM beside an ox-cart that carried his printing-press. Launched the *Saskatchewan Herald*, first newspaper in the Territories.**

Richard Laurie (1858–1938): **Son of P.G. Laurie; in 1884 became a partner with John Gowanlock in grist mill in Frog Lake. Served as a lieutenant in F Company, 90th Winnipeg Rifles, in General Middleton's column.**

Father Laurent Legoff, OMI: **Oblate priest at Cold Lake.**

Douglas Light (1933–2008): **Born in police barracks in Battleford, grandson of a NWMP constable and his Métis wife. Knew several surviving participants of 1885 events.**

Isabelle Little Bear Johns (1873–19?): **Daughter of Little Bear and granddaughter of Big Bear; was twelve years old and living in the Frog Lake camp at the time of the events of April 1885. Interviewed in 1958 through a Cree interpreter for *The Bonnyville Tribune*.**

James Grierson MacGregor (1905–1989): Author of numerous popular books on the subject of western-Canadian history such as *Peter Fidler: Canada's Forgotten Explorer* and a biography of Father Lacombe. Served a long term on the editorial board of *Alberta Historical Review* as well as governor of Glenbow Institute in Calgary.

Rod Macleod (1940–): Historian, editor, and author of military histories of the Canadian West such as *Swords and Ploughshares: War and Agriculture in Western Canada* and *The Mounties.*

David Mandelbaum (1911–1987): American anthropologist and author of *The Plains Cree: An Ethnographic, Historical and Comparative Study* and *Anthropology and People: The World of the Plains Cree.*

Nellie McClung (1873–1951): Suffragist, legislator, lecturer, social reformer, and author of such popular works as *In Times Like These* and *Sowing Seeds in Danny.* In 1929 she was one of the "Famous Five" who battled in the courts and legislatures to have women declared persons under the law.

William James McLean (1841–1929): Fur trader and factor with the Hudson's Bay Company at Fort Pitt. After the events of 1885, became chief trader at Fort Alexander, Manitoba, then served as chief trader in charge of the Lake Winnipeg district at Lower Fort Garry.

Elizabeth McLean (1869–?): Daughter of William McLean and Helen Hunter Murray; wrote an account of the events of 1885, particularly her family's experience as hostages of the Big Bear Band, as did her father, her sister Katherine, and her brother Duncan.

John Sheridan Milloy (19??–): Canadian historian of the Plains Cree, government policy and Canadian residential schools in such studies as *A Historical Overview of Indian-Government Relations, 1755–1940* and *The Plains Cree: A Preliminary Trade and Military Chronology, 1670–1870*.

Alexander Morris (1826–1889): Lieutenant governor of the North-West Territories from 1872 to 1876; as Queen's representative (1873 and 1876) signed on behalf of the Crown treaties three, four, five, and six.

Desmond Morton (1937–): Canadian historian, especially of the military, in such texts as *A Military History of Canada*, *Fight or Pay: Soldiers' Families in the Great War* and *New France and War*.

Charles Pelham Mulvany (1835–1885): Author of *The History of the North-West Rebellion of 1885*, drew extensively on the available military records of the campaign, newspaper reports, and first-hand accounts of soldiers in the field.

Frank Oliver (1853–1933): Edmonton newspaper publisher and politician; brought first printing press to Edmonton. Member of the North-West Council (1883–85) for Edmonton.

Lewis Redman Ord (1856–1942): Travelled to Edmonton in 1872 as part of survey party that went all over NWT. In 1885 he was a member of a survey corps attached to military units. Published *Reminiscences* anonymously in 1886.

Amelia M. Paget, née McLean (1867–1922): Eldest of twelve children of HBC factor William John McLean and Helen Hunter Murray, also of fur-trading stock. Gifted linguist of Native languages. In 1906, received commission from the Department of Indian

Affairs to travel among the Plains Indians and interview elders; published findings: *People of the Plains*, 1909.

John Pyne Pennefather (1833–1913): English medical doctor; served as surgeon to Major General T.B. Strange's column with the Alberta Field force.

Allen Ronaghan (1923–): Historian of western Canada.

Corporal R.B. Sleigh (?–1885): Member NWMP stationed at Frog Lake and Fort Pitt.

Norma Sluman (1924–): Biographer of Poundmaker and co-author with Jean Goodwill of *John Tootoosis: Biography of a Cree Leader*.

George F.G. Stanley (1907–2002): Historian, author, soldier, teacher, public servant, and designer of the Canadian flag.

George Stanley, Mesunekwepan (1868–?): Grandson of Chaschakiskwis, chief of Frog Lake Reserve at the signing of Treaty Six, and son of Ohneepahaow, chief at time of events in 1885 when Stanley was seventeen.

Sir Samuel "Sam" Benfield Steele (1849–1919): Skilful as a scout and tracker, he led a unit of Scouts of the NWMP as part of Strange's column of militia in pursuit of Big Bear's band.

Blair Stonechild (19??–): Member of the Muscowpetung First Nation in Saskatchewan, director of the Indian Studies department at the First Nations University of Canada, Regina, and historian of First Nations education and of Cree perspectives on the events of 1885.

Major General Thomas Bland Strange (1831–1925): **Retired British officer ranching near Calgary when contacted by the Minister of Defense to organize the Alberta Field Force, a group of local militia and NWMP officers in Middleton's army.**

Jim Thunder: **First Nations educator.**

Auguste-Henri de Trémaudan (1874–1929): **Resident in France, Saskatchewan, and Manitoba; collected numerous writings, rare documents, and oral testimonies about the history of the Métis.**

Bill Waiser (1953–): **Professor of history, University of Saskatchewan, author of *Saskatchewan: A New History* and *Who Killed Jackie Bates: Murder and Mercy During the Great Depression*.**

Constable C. Whitehead: **Member of the NWMP at Fort Battleford.**

Rudy Wiebe (1934–): **Edmonton writer of historic fictions of Mennonites and of Canadian First Nations and Métis history, notably *The Blue Mountains of China*, *The Temptations of Big Bear*, *A Stolen Life: The Journey of a Cree Woman* (with Yvonne Johnson), and *Of This Earth: A Mennonite Boyhood in the Boreal Forest*, and a biography, *Big Bear*.**

WORKS CITED

Adam, G. Mercer. *From Savagery to Civilization: The Canadian North-West: Its History and Its Troubles, From the Early Days of the Fur Trade etc.* Whitby, ON: Rose Publishing, 1885.

Adams, Howard. *Tortured People: The Politics of Colonization.* Penticton, BC: Theytus Books, 1999.

———. *Prison of Grass: Canada from the Native Point of View.* Toronto: New Press, 1975.

Beal, Bob and Robert Macleod. *Prairie Fire: The 1885 North-West Rebellion.* Edmonton, AB: Hurtig, 1984.

Begg, Alexander. *History of the North-West.* Vol. 3. Toronto: Hunter, Rose, 1895.

Boulton, Charles A. *Reminiscences of the North-West Rebellions: Commanding Boulton's Scouts.* Toronto: Grip, 1886. Available from http://wsb.datapro.net/rebellions

Breen, David. "'Timber Tom' and the North-West Rebellion", *Alberta Historical Review*, Vol. 19 (Summer 1971).

Brown, Wayne. *Steele's Scouts: Samuel Benfield Steele and the North-West Rebellion.* Surrey, BC: Heritage House, 2001.

Buck, Ruth, ed. *Voices of the Plains Cree.* Regina, SK: Canadian Plains Research Centre, 1995.

Cameron, William B. *Blood Red the Sun.* 1926. Reprint, Edmonton, AB: Hurtig, 1977.

Carter, Sarah. *Two Months in the Camp of Big Bear: The Life and Adventures of Theresa Gowanlock and Theresa Delaney.* Regina, SK: Canadian Plains Research Centre, 1999.

Charette, Guillaume. *Vanishing Spaces: Memoirs of Louis Goulet*. Translated by Ray Ellenwood. Winnipeg, MB: Éditions Bois-Brûlés, 1976.

Dagg, Mel. *The Women on the Bridge*. Saskatoon, SK: Thistledown, 1992.

Daoust, Charles R. *Cent-vingt jours de service actif: Récit de la campagne de 1885 du 65ème au Nord-ouest*, 1886. Reprint, St-Lambert, QC: Éditions numerus, 2006.

Delaney, Theresa and Theresa Gowanlock. *Two Months in the Camp of Big Bear*. Introduction by Sarah Carter. Regina, SK: Canadian Plains Research Centre, 1999.

Dempsey, Hugh A. *Big Bear: The End of Freedom*. Vancouver, BC: Douglas & McIntyre, 1984.

Dion, Alphonse. "A Redman's Viewpoint." In *Land of Red and White*. Heinsberg, AB: Frog Lake Community Club, 1977.

Dion, Joseph F. *My Tribe the Crees*. 1979. Reprint, Calgary, AB: Glenbow-Alberta Institute, 1996.

Donkin, John G. *Trooper in the Far North-West*. 1889. Reprint, Saskatoon, SK: Western Producer Prairie Books, 1987.

Elliott, David R. *Adventures in the West: Henry Ross Halpin, Fur Trader and Indian Agent*. Toronto: Natural Heritage Books, 2008.

Elliott, Lee. "Bewildered Inn." Unpublished.

Erasmus, Peter. *Buffalo Days and Nights*. Calgary, AB: Fifth House, 1999.

Feutl, Rita. "Frog Lake: Anniversary of a Massacre," *Edmonton Sun*, March 31, 1985.

Flanagan, Thomas. *Riel and the Rebellion: 1885 Reconsidered*, 2nd ed. Toronto: University of Toronto Press, 2000.

Fort Battleford-Post Journal. [Transcription of the original journal; no author cited]. Winnipeg, MB: Parks Canada, 1987.

Freeman, Lorraine. *The Largest Mass Hanging Since Confederation*. Available from www.metisresourcecentre.mb.ca

Fryer, Harold. *Frog Lake Massacre*. Surrey, BC: Heritage House, 1984.

Fulford, Robert. "Big Bear, Frog Lake, and My Aunt Theresa," *Saturday Night*, June 1976.

Gallaher, Bill. *The Frog Lake Massacre*. Surrey, BC: TouchWood Editions, 2008.

Goodwill, Jean and Norma Sluman. *John Tootoosis: A Biography of a Cree Leader*. Ottawa: Golden Dog, 1982.

Griesbach, W. A. *I Remember*. Toronto: Ryerson, 1946.

Hendriks, Robert. "Whose Cross is Whose, You Ask?" *Historic Trails Archive*. Available from www.ourheritage.net

———. *William Bleasdell Cameron: A Life of Writing and Adventure*. Edmonton, AB: Athabasca University Press, 2008.

Hildebrandt, Walter. "Marginal Notes." In *Sightings*. Dunvegan, ON: Cormorant Books, 1991.

"History of the Saskatchewan Uprising," *Winnipeg Daily Sun*, 1885.

Horse, John. "Frog Lake Reserves, Treaty No. 6." In *Land of Red and White*. Heinsberg, AB: Frog Lake Community Club, 1977.

Howard, Joseph. *Strange Empire: Louis Riel and the Metis People*. Toronto: James, Lewis, and Samuel, 1974.

Hughes, Stuart, ed. *The Frog Lake Massacre: Personal Perspectives on Ethnic Conflict*. Toronto: McClelland & Stewart, 1976.

"Indian Agent Mann 1885." In *Fort Pitt History Unfolding 1829–1925*. Frenchman Butte, SK: Frenchman Butte Fort Pitt Historical Society, 1985.

Jefferson, Robert. *Fifty Years on the Saskatchewan: Being a history of the Cree Indian domestic life and the difficulties which led to serious agitation and conflict of 1885 in the Battleford locality*. Vol. 1, No. 5, Canadian North-West Historical Society Publications. Battleford, SK: Canadian North-West Historical Society, 1929.

Jenish, D'arcy. *Indian Fall: The Last Great Days of the Plains Cree and the Blackfoot Confederacy*. Toronto: Penguin, 2000.

LaChance, Vernon. "Diary of Inspector Francis Dickens." In *Fort Pitt History Unfolding*. Frenchman Butte, SK: Fort Pitt Historical Society, 1985. Reprint of "The Diary of Francis Dickens." *Bulletin of the Departments of History and Political and Economic Science in Queen's University, Kingston, Ontario, Canada*, No. 59, May 1930.

Laurie, Richard C. *Reminiscences of Early Days in Battleford*. Battleford, SK: *Saskatchewan Herald*, 1935.

Legoff, Laurent. "During the Rebellion." In *The Frog Lake Massacre: Personal Perspectives on Ethnic Conflict*, edited by Stuart Hughes. Toronto: McClelland & Stewart, 1976.

——. "Fr Laurent Legoff, O.M.I. to Bishop Grandin." In *The Frog Lake Massacre: Personal Perspectives on Ethnic Conflict*, edited by Stuart Hughes. Toronto: McClelland & Stewart, 1976.

Light, Douglas. *Footprints in the Dust*. North Battleford, SK: Turner-Warwick, 1987.

Little Bear Johns, Isabelle. "Memoirs of a Cree Woman." Reprint from *The Bonnyville Tribune*, 1958. *Edmonton Sunday Sun*, March 31, 1985.

MacGregor, James G. *Blankets and Beads: A History of the Saskatchewan River*. Edmonton, AB: Institute of Applied Art, 1949.

McClung, Nellie. *Clearing in the West: My Own Story*. 1935. Reprint, Toronto: Thomas Allen, 1964.

McLean, Duncan. "The Last Hostage." In *Frog Lake Massacre*, edited by Harold Fryer. Frontier Books, 32. Surrey, BC: Heritage House, 1984.

McLean, Elizabeth. "The Siege of Fort Pitt." In *The Frog Lake Massacre: Personal Perspectives on Ethnic Conflict*, edited by Stuart Hughes. Toronto: McClelland & Stewart, 1976.

———. "Prisoners of the Indians." In *The Frog Lake Massacre: Personal Perspectives on Ethnic Conflict*, edited by Stuart Hughes. Toronto: McClelland & Stewart, 1976.

———. "Our Captivity Ended." In *The Frog Lake Massacre: Personal Perspectives on Ethnic Conflict*, edited by Stuart Hughes. Toronto: McClelland & Stewart, 1976.

McLean, William J. "Tragic Events at Frog Lake and Fort Pitt During the North West Rebellion." In *The Frog Lake Massacre: Personal Perspectives on Ethnic Conflict*, edited by Stuart Hughes. Toronto: McClelland & Stewart, 1976.

Mandelbaum, David G. *The Plains Cree: An Ethnographic, Historical, and Comparative Study*. Regina, SK: Canadian Plains Research Centre, 1979.

Midland Historical Volunteers 1885. *Battalion History and Chronology of 1885*. Available at http://www.geocities.com/yosemite/forest/8889/

Milloy, John S. *The Plains Cree: Trade, Diplomacy and War, 1790 to 1870*. Winnipeg, MB: University of Manitoba Press, 1990.

Morris, Alexander. *Treaties of Canada with the Indians of Manitoba and the North-West Territories: including the Negotiations on which they were based and other information relating thereto*. 1880. Reprint, Calgary, AB: Fifth House, 1991.

Mulvany, Charles Pelham. *The History of the North-West Rebellion: Comprising a full and impartial account of the origin and progress of the war. Including a history of the Indian tribes of North-Western Canada*. Toronto: A. H. Hovey, 1885.

Oliver, Frank. *Edmonton Bulletin*, July 18, 1885.

Ord, Lewis Redman. *Reminiscences of a Bungle by One of the Bunglers*, edited by Rod C. Macleod. Edmonton, AB: University of Alberta Press, 1983.

Paget, Amelia M. *The People of the Plains*. Regina, SK: Canadian Plains Research Centre, 2004.

Pennefather, John P. *Thirteen Years on the Prairies: From Winnipeg to Cold Lake, fifteen hundred miles*. London, UK: K. Paul, Trench, Trubner, 1892.

Ronaghan, Allen. "Who Was the 'Fine Young man'? The Frog Lake Massacre Revisited." *Saskatchewan History*, Fall 1995.

Sleigh, R.B. "Diary of Corporal R.B. Sleigh, NWMP Frog Lake." In *History of the Saskatchewan Uprising*. [Typescript]. *Winnipeg Daily Sun*, 1885.

Stanley, George. F.G. *The Birth of Western Canada: A History of the Riel Rebellions*. 1930. Reprint, Toronto: University of Toronto Press, 1970.

Stanley, George. "An Account of the Frog Lake Massacre." In *The Frog Lake Massacre: Personal Perspectives on Ethnic Conflict*, edited by Stuart Hughes. Toronto: McClelland & Stewart, 1976.

Steele, Samuel Benfield. *Forty Years in Canada: Reminiscences of the Great Northwest*. Toronto: McClelland, Goodchild & Stewart, 1915.

Stobie, Margaret R. *The Other Side of Rebellion*. Edmonton, AB: NeWest Press, 1986.

Stonechild, Blair. *Saskatchewan Indians and the Resistance of 1885: Two Case Studies*. Regina, SK: Saskatchewan Education, 1986.

Stonechild, Blair and Bill Waiser. *Loyal Till Death: Indians and the North-West Rebellion*. Calgary, AB: Fifth House, 1997.

"Story Told by Jimmy Chief." In *Fort Pitt History Unfolding 1829–1925*. Frenchman Butte, SK: Fort Pitt Historical Society, 1985.

Strange, Thomas Bland. *Gunner Jingo's Jubilee*. 1893. Reprint, Edmonton, AB: Hurtig, 1988.

——. *The Story of Riel's Revolt. Canada: 1885, Part ii*. Available at www.gaslight.mtroyal.ca/revoltx2.htm

Thunder, Jim. "Battle at Frenchman Butte 1885." *Saskatchewan Indian*, August 1985.

Trémaudan, Auguste-Henri de. *Histoire de la Nation Métisse dans l'ouest Canadien*. Montreal: Éditions Albert Lévesque, 1935.

Wiebe, Rudy. *The Temptations of Big Bear*. Toronto: McClelland & Stewart, 1973.

FURTHER READING

Audet, Shawna. *Riel Rebellion Story: The Frog Lake Massacre.* Available at
http://mapleleafpro.net/storyriel.html

Bjarnason, Dan. "Public Hanging for Frog Lake Massacre." CBC *Digital Archive.*
Available at http://archives.cbc.ca/society/crime_justice/clips/3346/

Brennan, Brian. *Scoundrels and Scallywags: Characters from Alberta's Past.* Calgary,
AB: Fifth House, 2002.

Campbell, Maria. "She Who Knows the Truth of Big Bear: History calls him
traitor, but history sometimes lies." *Maclean's,* September 1975.

Carter, Sarah. *Capturing Women: The Manipulation of Cultural Imagery in
Canada's Prairie West.* Montreal-Kingston: McGill-Queen's University
Press, 1997.

———. *Lost Harvests: Prairie Indian Reserve Farmers and Government Policy.*
Montreal-Kingston: McGill-Queen's University Press, 1990.

Daoust, Charles R. *One Hundred and Twenty Days of Active Service: A complete
historical narrative of the campaign of the 65th in the North West.* Translation
of *Cent-vingt jours de service actif.* 1886. Reprint, St-Lambert, QC: Éditions
Numerus, 2006.

"Frog Lake Massacre." *Encyclopedia of Saskatchewan.* Available at http://esask.
uregina.ca/entry/frog_lake_massacre.html.

The Frog Lake Massacre: The Killings That Set the West Afire. Available at
 http://firstpeoplesofcanada.com/fp_metis/fp_metis_frog_lake.html

Hildebrandt, Walter. *Views From Fort Battleford: Constructed Visions of an
 Anglo-Canadian West*. Reprint, Regina, SK: Canadian Plains Research
 Centre, 2009.

MacEwan, Grant. *Portraits from the Plains*. Toronto: McGraw-Hill, 1971.

McCoy, Edward James. *"A Lesson They Would Not Soon Forget": The Convicted
 Native Participants of the 1885 North-West Rebellion*. MA thesis, University
 of Calgary, 2002.

Miller, Robert. *Frog Lake: A Spring of Blood*. Warburg, AB: Tipi Publishers, 2006.

Morton, Desmond. *The Last War Drum: The North West Campaign of 1885*.
 Toronto: A. M. Hakkert, 1972.

Siggins, Maggie. *Riel: A Life of Revolution*. Toronto: HarperCollins, 1994.

Stonechild, Blair. "The Indian View of the 1885 Uprising." In *1885 and After:
 Native Society in Transition*. Eds. F. Laurie Barron & James B. Waldram.
 Regina, SK: Canadian Plains Research Centre, 1986.

The Trials/Role of Indians in the 1885 Uprising. Regina, SK: Gabriel Dumont
 Institute of Native Studies and Applied Research.

The Virtual Museum of Métis History and Culture. Gabriel Dumont Institute of
 Native Studies and Applied Research. Available at www.metismuseum.ca

Wiebe, Rudy. *Big Bear*. Toronto: Penguin Canada, 2008.

PERMISSIONS

Excerpts from Howard Adams' *Prison of Grass: Canada from the Native Point of View* were reprinted with kind permission from Margaret Adams.

Excerpts from Edward Ahenakew's (author) and Ruth Buck's (editor) *Voices of the Plains Cree*, Sarah Carter's introduction to *Two Months in the Camp of Big Bear: The Life and Adventures of Theresa Gowanlock and Theresa Delaney*, and David G. Mandelbaum's *The Plains Cree: An Ethnographic, Historical, and Comparative Study* were reprinted with permission from the Canadian Plains Research Centre.

Excerpts from Bob Beal and Robert Macleod's *Prairie Fire: The 1885 North-West Rebellion* were reprinted with kind permission from Bob Beal.

Excerpts from David Breen's article "'Timber Tom' and the North-West Rebellion" were reprinted with kind permission from the author.

Within are excerpts from *Steele's Scouts: Samuel Benfield Steele and the North-West Rebellion*. Copyright © 2001 by Peter Wayne Brown. Reprinted by permission of Heritage House Publishing Co. Ltd.

Within are excerpts from *The Women on the Bridge* by Mel Dagg (Thistledown Press, 1992). Reprinted by permission of the publisher.

Excerpts from *Big Bear: The End of Freedom* by Hugh Dempsey, published in 2006 by Douglas & McIntyre, were reprinted with permission from the publisher.

Excerpts from Joseph Dion's *My Tribe the Crees* and Peter Erasmus' *Buffalo Days and Nights* were reprinted with permission from the Glenbow Museum.

Excerpts from David Elliott's *Adventure in the West: Henry Halpin, Fur Trader and Indian Agent* were reprinted with permission from Dundurn Press Ltd. Copyright © 2008.

The unpublished poem "Bewildered Inn" by Lee Elliott was reprinted with kind permission from the author.

Excerpts from Rita Feutl's article "Frog Lake: Anniversary of a Massacre" were reprinted with permission from Sun Media Corporation.

Excerpts from Thomas Flanagan's *Riel and the Rebellion: 1885 Reconsidered* and George F.G. Stanley's *The Birth of Western Canada: A History of the Riel Rebellions* were reprinted with permission from the University of Toronto Press.

Excerpts from *Fort Pitt History Unfolding* were reprinted with permission from the Fort Pitt Historical Society.

Excerpts from Lorraine Freeman's *The Largest Mass Hanging Since Confederation* were reprinted with permission from the Métis Cultural and Heritage Resource Centre.

Excerpts from Robert Fulford's article "Big Bear, Frog Lake, and My Aunt Theresa" were reprinted with kind permission from the author.

Excerpts from *The Frog Lake Massacre* by Bill Gallaher, 2008, were reprinted with permission from TouchWood Editions, www.touchwoodeditions.com.

Excerpts from Robert Hendriks' article "Whose Cross is Whose, You Ask?" were reprinted with kind permission from the author.

Excerpts from Walter Hildebrandt's "Marginal Notes" were reprinted with permission from the author.

Excerpts from *Indian Fall: The Last Great Days of the Plains Cree and Blackfoot Confederacy* were reprinted with kind permission from D'arcy Jenish.

Excerpts from Douglas Light's *Footprints in the Dust* were reprinted with kind permission from Meriel Light.

Excerpts from John S. Milloy's *The Plains Cree: Trade, Diplomacy, and War, 1790 to 1870* were reprinted with permission from the University of Manitoba Press.

Excerpts from Lewis Redman Ord's *Reminiscences of a Bungle by One of the Bunglers*, edited by Rod C. Macleod were reprinted with kind permission from the University of Alberta Press.

Excerpts from Allen Ronaghan's article "Who Was That Fine Young Man? The Frog Lake Massacre Revisited" were reprinted with kind permission from the author.

Excerpts from Blair Stonechild's *Saskatchewan Indians and the Resistance of 1885: Two Case Studies* were reprinted with kind permission from the author.

Within are excerpts from *The Temptations of Big Bear* by Rudy Wiebe. Copyright © 1973 by Rudy Wiebe. Reprinted by permission of Knopf Canada for Canadian and UK rights, and of Swallow Press/Ohio University Press, Athens, Ohio, www.ohioswallow.com, for US rights.

A Republishing Transactional Licence Agreement was obtained from Access Copyright for reprinting excerpts from the following:

Vanishing Spaces: Memoirs of a Prairie Métis by Guillaume Charette. Copyright © 1980 by Pemmican Publications.

John Tootoosis: Biography of a Cree Leader by Jean Goodwill and Norma Sluman. Copyright © 1984 by Pemmican Publications.

Permission from the Copyright Board of Canada was obtained for reprinting excerpts from the following:

Alphonse Dion's "A Redman's Viewpoint" in *Land of Red and White*.

Harold Fryer's *Frog Lake Massacre*.

John Horse's "Frog Lake Reserves, Treaty No. 6" in *Land of Red and White*.

Stuart Hughes' *The Frog Lake Massacre: Personal Perspectives on Ethnic Conflict*.

James G. MacGregor's *Blankets and Beads: A History of the Saskatchewan River*.

Margaret R. Stobie's *The Other Side of Rebellion*.

Jim Thunder's "Battle at Frenchman Butte 1885" in *Saskatchewan Indian*.

Other excerpts were reprinted from Public Domain.

INDEX

¶ The display typeface is Albertan, designed and cut in metal at the 16 pt. size by Jim Rimmer in 1982.

¶ The text face is ʟᴛᴄ Kaatskill, which was originally designed by Frederic Goudy and later completed by Jim Rimmer for the Lanston Type Company.

¶ The sans serif is Robert Slimbach's Cronos Pro.

Born and raised in Edmonton, Alberta, award-winning nonfiction writer Myrna Kostash is the author of nine books, including *All of Baba's Children* and *The Doomed Bridegroom: A Memoir*. In addition to contributing articles to various magazines, such as *Geist*, *Canadian Geographic*, and *Legacy*, Kostash has written radio documentaries and theatre playscripts. Her creative nonfiction has appeared in numerous Canadian and international anthologies, such as *The Thinking Heart: Best Canadian Essays*, *Edmonton on Location*, *Literatura na Świecie* (Warsaw), and *Mostovi* (Belgrade).

A founder of the Creative Nonfiction Collective, Kostash has taught creative writing workshops across Canada and in the US. She has served on several award juries, including those of the Governor General's Awards, the CBC Creative Nonfiction competition, and the Writers' Trust Non-Fiction Prize. In 2008 the Writers Guild of Alberta presented her with the Golden Pen Award for lifetime achievement, and in 2009 she was inducted into the City of Edmonton's Arts and Culture Hall of Fame. Her upcoming book, *Prodigal Daughter: A Journey into Byzantium*, will be released in 2010.